SCIENTIFIC MANAGEMENT OF FOREST LIBRARIES

Vinod Kumar
I.F.S.

2018
Daya Publishing House®
A Division of
Astral International Pvt. Ltd.
New Delhi - 110 002

First Published, 1998
Reprinted, 2018

ISBN: 978-81-7035-194-8 (Hardbound)

Publisher's note:

Every possible effort has been made to ensure that the information contained in this book is accurate at the time of going to press, and the publisher and author cannot accept responsibility for any errors or omissions, however caused. No responsibility for loss or damage occasioned to any person acting, or refraining from action, as a result of the material in this publication can be accepted by the editor, the publisher or the author. The Publisher is not associated with any product or vendor mentioned in the book. The contents of this work are intended to further general scientific research, understanding and discussion only. Readers should consult with a specialist where appropriate.

Every effort has been made to trace the owners of copyright material used in this book, if any. The author and the publisher will be grateful for any omission brought to their notice for acknowledgement in the future editions of the book.

Published by : **Daya Publishing House®**
A Division of
Astral International Pvt. Ltd.
– ISO 9001:2008 Certified Company –
4736/23, Ansari Road, Darya Ganj
New Delhi-110 002
Ph. 011-43549197, 23278134
E-mail: info@astralint.com
Website: www.astralint.com

PREFACE

The field of Forestry science and literature has witnessed tremendous developments during the past few decades. However, all the informations developed and gathered in the field of forestry is not being read and utilized by the foresters as well as people who are engaged in tree planting activities. The main reason being that the forest libraries have not been able to serve the users in a proper way. The forest libraries are not maintained properly due to variety of reasons. The librarian or the library-in-charge also have not been able to work as informaticians.

The information is a vital resource and is an essential input for enhanced productivity in forestry research and development. Over the years there has been an exponential growth in forestry information. Besides, new developments in environmental technology have resulted in introducing information services based on computers and computer media. A well equipped information centre is an essential part of any organisation if it has to survive as a viable successful entity.

The librarian or the person looking after the library presently does not know the extent of literature that he is having in the forest library. The cataloguing is utterly poor or absent and it is very difficult to know the documents available on a particular subject. The valuable knowledge accumulated so far has vanished or remained in the dark due to the poor performance of the forest libraries.

The time has come to take maximum advantage of the forestry material available if the mother earth is to be reclothed with trees and this is possible only when libraries would be developed and used on a scientific basis by using the OXFORD SYSTEM OF DECIMAL CLASSIFICATION FOR FORESTRY as a tool for classification and cataloguing. The use of ODC will lead to qualitative improvement of existing library and information services. It will become possible to improve the library services through the application of ODC and related information technology which are difficult to provide otherwise. It can finally be said that academic track will change from narrow gauge to broad gauge.

For a long time it has been felt that a book should be published to acquaint the forester and scientist community with the resources and facilities that can be made available in the Forest libraries so that these facilities can better be utilized for forestry development. This book will make the scientists and foresters aware of various procedures and information services that can be had from the different forest libraries. The forest libraries should be reader oriented and should follow the open access system.

The attempt should also be made to create computer culture in the forest libraries.

I wish to thank Shri U.P. Dhotekar, Range Forest Officer and Shri B. F. Ambekar, Steno for their kind cooperation and hard work, in typing and checking the manuscript.

I am also obliged to my wife and children for great cooperation and encouragement.

Chandrapur
Maharashtra

Dt. 11th. September 1997

VINOD KUMAR
Indian Forest Service

Contents

1

Introduction and Present Status of Forest Libraries in the Department

Introduction

According to the Oxford English dictionary, as early as 1374, the term 'Library' was employed in English to refer to a place where books were kept for "reading, study or reference". By the nineteenth century a library was also regarded as "a building, room, or set of rooms containing a collection of books for the use of the public or some portion of it, or the member of a society. The modern library can be said as a public institution or establishment charged with the care of a collection of books." In this definition the emphasis is on the care of the collection, whereas the role of user of human being is missing from it.

The American Library Association glossary of library and information science has defined library as "a collection of materials organized to provide physical, bibliographic and intellectual access to a target group, with a staff that is trained to provide services and programmes related to the information needs of the target groups."

The libraries have been an essential part of civilized society. These came into being to serve the needs of the society. The libraries have played an important part in the social, political, economic and cultural development of the society. With the passage of time, communication of knowledge has become increasingly important. The knowledge has become increasingly complex and at the same time means of communication of knowledge are also becoming equally complex. The library has helped in communication of knowledge by providing repackaged information through user services.

We are living in the information age. Information plays an important and crucial role in the advancement of knowledge, decision making, planning, avoidance of duplication of effects and technology transfer. A Forest Researcher would need information to keep himself up to date and well informed in the field of forestry. Research provides solutions to many problems. In the changing environment modern libraries are no longer mere depositories of all past, present and future knowledge. In fact, these have become information oriented. The modern libraries acquire variety of items including books, periodical publications, microforms, slides, photographs, audiocassettes, video-cassettes, maps, models, artifacts (man-made objects), realia (natural objects such as geological specimens), gramophone records, tape records etc. In the context of a library, these things may be called **documents**.

Functions of Library

A library is a social institution and therefore it is expected to perform certain functions. The functions of a library are:

(a) Life-long self education.

(b) Information/documents on various subjects to serve economic, political and social welfare.

(c) Proper use of leisure.

(d) Advancement of culture.

(e) Preservation and development of scientific knowledge.

LAWS OF LIBRARY SCIENCE

Dr. S. R. Ranganathan had formulated narrative principles of library science consisting of laws, canons and principles as below :

Law : In the context of a major discipline, such as Library Science.

Canon : In the context of divisions of the first order of a major discipline, such as book selection, classification, and cataloguing.

Principle : In the context of division of the second or later order of the major discipline such as facet sequence in classification and alphabetization in cataloguing.

Dr. S. R. Ranganathan formulated *Five laws of library science in 1928 which are as under :*

(i) Books are for use (First law of library science) : Its aim is to enable the users to make the most effective use of the resources and services of the library rather than preservation. A modern library feels satisfied only if the users keep on emptying the shelves constantly. It is expected to convert potential users into habitual users by allowing open access to books. The books should be selected and acquired keeping in view the present and potential requirements of users. Purchase of costly books which are not likely to be in frequent demand should be avoided.

(ii) Every readers his/her book (second law of library science) : Here emphasis is on reader meaning thereby that "Books are for all". In order to meet this goal, it is desirable that economic factor should not stand as barrier. This law provides that free library service should be provided to all. The book selection needs to be done judiciously so the collection meets demands of the users adequately. The subject(s), language (s) and style of exposition of books to be selected should be closely related to the requirements of the users. A book selector must select books to save the requirements of different categories of users. The second law suggests the formation of a national library net-work to share the resources especially for the purpose of inter-library loan.

(iii) Every book its reader (Third law of library science) : This law desires that every book in a library must find its reader. It implies that there would be maximum use of books by their users. Do not select books in language (s), subject (s) and level (s) for which there are not going to be many users. For books which are required occasionally, one should depend on inter-library loan.

The books should be arranged so that every book finds a reader or the possibility for getting a reader should be very high. In open access, users should not be allowed to replace books on shelves as users are more likely to misplace books. A misplaced book is virtually a lost book. The chances of securing a reader for a misplaced book are minimum. Thus shelf rectification should be carried out frequently to restore misplaced books.

(iv) Save the time of the reader (Fourth law of library science) : Since a user is a busy person his time must be saved. This law revolves around the users. A corrollary to this fourth law is "save the time of the staff". A user interested in silviculture will also like to browse books in the field of mensuration or utilisation, therefore, these subjects should be arranged side by side. The alphabetical arrangement of subjects is unhelpful and time consuming. The absolute position of various subjects must be kept in view. In a stack room, books in subjects having least demand must be ordinarily shelved at the farthest portion of the stack room. This will result in broken order of books but will lead to saving of time of the users. Similarly the ready reference books which are in great demand are kept at the reference desk whereby time of the users can be saved. The same arrangements are applicable for displaying "latest additions" near the entrance of the library. The catalogue must be prepared by a qualified professional cataloguer. Who knows the job thoroughly. The library services should be so planned and organised that a user is able to get information/documents required by him promptly. Signs in the form of various guides serve a very useful purpose in a stack room. There should be a general guide affixed at the entrance of the stack, which should give an overall view of the arrangement of books in the stacks.

(v) A library is a growing organism (fifth law of Library science) : As library is a social institution, it should keep on growing like an organism. A library should grow in terms of documents, readers and staff. The old books should be replaced by new books in order to attract more and more users. In order to maintain live collection, a library must procure new books and journals. Library building must be planned keeping in view the present and future needs. There should be provision for repository warehouses to accommodate less used materials. It is essential that weeding of documents should be carried out regularly to achieve a live collection. The dynamic character of the collection should be maintained by adding new documents to take care of the readers being served. When a library grows, sanctioned staff at some stage would become inadequate. In order to provide effective services, it would be necessary to increase the staff.

The first three laws emphasizes the exploitation of the document of the library fully by the maximum number of users. The role of a reference librarian is extremely important towards satisfying the requirements of fourth law. This law provides to the users variety of library and information services so that their time can be saved and administration and management of libraries can be revolutionized. The four-laws are over-enthusiastic but the fifth law puts a restraint on these. The central theme of these laws is a 'user' who is regarded as all important.

Present Status of Forest Libraries

Generally the libraries are small and are maintained and used in a causal way. It is now realized that for quicker socio-economic development, it is not only necessary to promote-scientific and technological research but also to disseminate information at a faster pace to the users. The library and documentation centre plays a vital role for dissemination of information to their target scientists of research organizations. Thus the library and documentation centre has to be considered the back-bone of any socio-economic development. So is the case with our libraries.

The status of libraries in the department as they exist today can be summarised as below :—

(1) All the Research Centres, Dy. C. F. and C. F. Offices have libraries but they are hardly maintained in a nice way. There is no separate building or spacious room for the library.

(2) The libraries do not contain sufficient cup-boards, display-racks, reading tables, reading chairs, catalogues etc. to keep volumes of book-properly in the libraries.

(3) The libraries do not contain the books, booklets, catalogues etc. with latest amendments.

(4) The libraries consist of most of the books which are in English which do not cater to the lower forest staff who understand mostly books in local language.

(5) There is no provision for translating good works from English to local language and therefore the subordinate staff is not aware of the knowledge of the latest developments in Forestry.

(6) The libraries are being looked after by a RFO, Forester, Forest guard, accountant or by a clerk who is not trained in the Library Science or library procedures. The lack of staff and knowl-

edge in library science has resulted in poor maintenance of the library, poor cataloguing and classification etc.

(7) The funds for the purchase of books, periodicals and equipments for the libraries are poorly available. The number of books and periodicals are not sufficient and upto date. The important books are hardly purchased in sufficient numbers.

(8) Power to purchase books, periodicals etc. is also limited.

(9) The subordinate staff is not motivated to read the literature in forestry. Only few selected gazetted staff often use the library facilities.

2

Introduction to Classification

Classification Systems

The several classification systems that exist can be enumerated as under :

(1) **Special** : Used for covering a particular subject or laying emphasis on it.

(2) **Scientific** : Used for systematic study of the phenomena of the natural world.

(3) **General** : This system is used for displaying all recorded knowledge or the universe of information.

This is further sub-divided as below :—

(a) ***Enumerative Classification*** : Comprises categories in which the universe of knowledge is divided and exhaustively listed.

(b) ***Faceted or analytical-Synthetic Classification*** : Characteristics common to many categories are identified. These are then arranged into lists (or tables) each of which represents a facet. Subjects are thus analysed into their elements, which can later be recombined or synthesised by the user.

(c) ***Aspect Classification*** : Phenomena of the natural world are classified against the perspective of discipline or context in which they appear.

(4) **Documentary** : Used for the management of documents for

easy location and retrieval of information contained in them. This can be further divided into two categories as under :—

(a) ***Library Classification*** : Used for physical arrangement of library holdings and guidance to their contents.

(b) ***Bibliographic Classification*** : Used for description and indexing of documents in general and not restricted to any particular collection.

Classification Schemes

There are seven major and minor classification schemes that now exist and are worth mentioning—

(1) Dewey Decimal Classification (DDC), - 1876.

(2) Universal Decimal Classification (UDC) - 1987.

(3) Library of Congress Classification (LCC), 1901.

(4) Bibliographic Classification of Bliss (BD) 1910/1935.

(5) Colon Classification (BBK) - 1933.

(6) Library - Bibliographical Classification (BBK) - 1960.

(7) Rangnathan colon classification.

Out of these seven schemes only DDC and UDC are relevant as the "Oxford System of Decimal Classification for Forestry" has been derived from this. The DDC and UDC are closely linked with the "Oxford system of Decimal Classification for Forestry". The impact of computers on the UDC has been perceptible in various literary activities like computerised bibliographical and abstracting services, production of subject indexes, information retrieval and SDI, (Selective Dissemination of Information). The Computerisation has been possible due to its having structured and expressive notations which others do not possess. The UDC has been published in twenty three languages of the world.

The Classification Research Group (CRG) of U.K. formed in 1952 is responsible for the faceted scheme which is supposed to break a new ground. This scheme is based on the facet analytico of Ranganathan. The Universal Decimal Classification Scheme is in fact, the first analysis - synthetic scheme which displays faceted structure. The Colon Classification (1933) in which analysis has found practical application to a minute detail, is said to have, in turn, drawn its inspiration from U.D.C. Scheme.

The details of various systems, Facet analysis, Facet Formula etc. are beyond the limit of this book.

In Colon Classification, the so-called fundamental categories are pre-fixed as PMEST or personality, matter, energy, space and time. The limited number of fundamental categories reflected in the facet formula PMEST, imposes a hindrance to classification of subjects with more facets and this could be overcome through the Postulates of Levels and Rounds to fundamental categories of colon classification (CC). Therefore limiting the number of fundamental categories to five, as in the earlier editions of CC, a larger number of facets in a subject can be accommodated in it by repeating some of PMEST round and round. It can not be helped if this idea appears to be a complex one to many users.

Dewey System

The main classes of the DDC forms the base of the UDC. Melvil Dewey, the originator of the DDC, was born on December 10, 1851 at Adams centre, New York. He graduated from the Amherst College in 1874 and was posted as an Acting Librarian there. The DDC was devised by him for use in the Amherst College Library. It was first published in 1876. He became the Librarian of Columbia College New York city in 1883. Then he established the school of library economy which was the first institution for training librarians. He became the Director of the New York State Library (1889-1906) and also the State Director of libraries (1904-06). Under his guidance the state library, thoroughly organised, had the distinction of being the most efficient one in the United States. He had introduced the system of travelling libraries and picture collection. He was one of the founder of the American Library Association. Dewey died on December 26, 1931 at Lake Placid.

The DDC : The first edition entitled 'Classification and Subject Index' was published by Melvil Dewey in 1876, with 919 headings, it had no decimal fractions and was not called 'Decimal'. Class numbers with three digits minimum and decimal point after the third digit were introduced and the scheme was extended in successive editions. The DDC is basically a schedule of simple numerical notations representing subjects for arranging documents in a logical proximity in libraries. In the course of time, the gulf between the DDC and UDC had widened. But the main classes and their basic features have not altered except for the fact that the latest UDC schedule published in 1895, has perceptibly deviated in form from its earlier editions. The main classes therein had undergone changes. The division of the universe of knowledge into ten main classes in the DDC has been the subject of criticism from many quarters.

The DDC is the hierarchical system of classification where in the divisions and sub-divisions of classes proceeds from genus to species by stages. These divisions and sub-divisions are brought together by decimal notation. The Dewey system encompasses all recorded knowledge into ten main classes. These main classes are numbered 0-9. Each of these main classes is, in turn divided into ten divisions, and then each of these divisions into ten sections. The system gets its name from the sustained application of decimal point which divides each of these classes and their sub-divisions by ten.

The primary purpose of classification is two fold i.e. storage and retrieval of information and arrangement of documents on shelves. As all the subjects of documents are classified by the DDC whatever be their format or languages, a wide range of documents and media, including music records, discs cassettes, microfilms, photocopies, photographs, letters etc. can be classified by it.

The revision programme of the DDC is effected by the Decimal Classification Editorial Policy Committee, and a Joint Committee of the American Library Association (ALA) and Lake Placid Foundation. They advise the Forest Press on matters which are considered to be of interest to the users of the DDC. The notation of the DDC with its easily comprehensible Arabic numerals have proved itself to be an ideal tool for identification, location and retrieval of documents. It can be compared to shorthand notations which pack words through a limited number of symbols. The DDC is the oldest and most commonly used system which has been adopted by most of the Nations of the World. Its use is widespread in majority of libraries in English-speaking Countries.

Universal Decimal Classification System (UDC)

After the approval of the Lake Placid Education Foundation (New York) the proprietors of the Dewey Decimal Classification, and at the request of the British Society for International Bibliography (BSIB) and the Association of Special Libraries and Information Bureau (ASLIB), the British Standards Institution (BSI) has prepared the Universal Decimal Classification (UDC) International medium edition. The 1985 (FID Publication No. 571) replaces the abridged edition of 1961. The BISB and ASLIB have now been amalgamated as the ASLIB. The official language for the maintenance of UDC are English, French, and German. The UDC schedules are used for the classification of books and documents in about one hundred thousand libraries and information centres all over the world. The UDC has been adopted by the International Organisation for Standardisation (ISO) which has recommended it for the classification of published standards.

As the UDC is based on DDC, the UDC can also be deemed as documentary classification. Resulting from the fusion of principles of more than one form of classification, the UDC has developed into an instrument for subject identification, indexing and description of documents belonging to any particular collection or those existing independently.

The main structure of the UDC has been originally taken from the Dewey Decimal Classification (DDC) but it differs from the latter in respect of its auxiliary notation of distinctive symbols. With the help of these auxiliaries, complex subjects can be designated, classified and retrieved in terms of their component features. These features can be classified independently. Thus the need for repeated enumeration of similar concepts in different subject fields are substantially reduced. The UDC is kept up-to-date with advance in all fields of knowledge with the help of an international network of UDC revision committees. The UDC, which is maintained through a network of organisations and individuals, is truly international in character and coverage.

Meaning of Connotations

Class : These are main classes or tables with primary notation existing in the form of single-digit classes. The latest schedule of 1985 for U D C contains nine classes.

The example of class is

5 - Mathematics and Natural Science.

Sub-Class : Each of the ten theoretical classes of the earlier UDC schedule (or nine classes of the latest schedule) are divided to form ten narrower classes (or sub class).

These are two-digit classes.

For example - 51 mathematics.

Sub-divisions : These are three digit numbers derived from two digit sub-classes.

For example-514 Geometry.

Simple number : A number, either a main number or an independent auxiliary, when taken from a single place in the tables and cited on its own is a simple number.

For example - Theory of functions.

Compound Subject : In a compound subject, more than one element within a conventional class gets reflected.

For example - 565.2 : 65.011.4 - Economic efficiency of rail transport.

Compound Number : It is a number created by synthesis, using elements from more than one place in any distinct class of the table.

For example-681. 883. 4.04 Range of Sonar equipment.

Main Classes of UDC : The UDC consists of main and auxiliary tables. The main tables represent primary notation which reflects its close relation with the DDC. In this DDC, the main classes are denoted by 3 digits, while a single digit represents the main classes of the UDC. These main classes of UDC, are :

0 — Generalities, Science and Knowledge, Organisation, Information etc.

1 — Philosophy, Psychology.

2 — Religion, Theology.

3 — Social Sciences, Law, Government etc.

4 — Vacant.

5 — Mathematics and natural sciences.

6 — Applied sciences, Medicine, Technology.

7 — The Arts, Recreation, Entertainment, Sport.

3 — Language, Linguistics, Literature.

9 — Geography, Biography, History.

Previously, class 4 represented linguistics. It was cancelled in 1963, and the subject was merged with the class 8 Literature. Class 4 is now vacant.

These broadest or main classes are further divided into sub-classes which are shown by two-digit numbers. These numbers represent more restricted concepts. e.g. class 6 is divided as follows :

60 — General matters. Inventions.
61 — Medical Sciences.
62 — Engineering, Technology in general.
63 — Agriculture and related sciences and techniques.
64 — House keeping, House economics.
65 — Management and organisation of industry trade communications.
66 — Chemical technology, Chemical and related industries.
67 — Various industries, trades and crafts.
68 — Finished or assembled articles. Precision mechanisms.
69 — Building trade, materials, practice etc.

These two-digit classes are further sub-divided yielding three digit classes which represent even more restrictive concepts. As the process of division continues, the concepts get more and more restrictive till they are theoretically exhausted. The division of main tables follows a hierarchical pattern with the broadest classes at the highest level and the more restrictive classes at the lowest level.

The innovative feature of the UDC is its auxiliary notation comprising signs which allows for the construction or synthesis of compound numbers with the help of devices provided in the schedule. When a class number is created by synthesis of elements taken from different places in the schedule, the resultant number is known as the compound number. Auxiliary notations consist of two categories i.e. common auxiliaries and special auxiliaries. These are different from a simple number which occurs at any place in the schedule or as an independent auxiliary cited on its own.

Common Auxiliaries : The common auxiliaries establish inter-relations between subjects. The common auxiliaries consist of two kinds of symbols i.e. signs and sub-divisions.

The common auxiliary signs are a number of symbols which relate UDC numbers by linking them through co-ordination and aggregation to denote compound numbers.

The common auxiliary sub-divisions differ from auxiliary signs in two respects; firstly these comprise numeric tables, and similar to the main tables, concepts in it are enumerated and the arrangement is hierarchical. Secondly these concepts are followed, preceded by or prefixed to common auxiliary signs.

These common sub-divisions can theoretically be attached to very class number in the main table for denoting any concept in the scheme more specifically. When these sub-divisions are isolated and cited independently, the characteristics of division can be identified by the addition of an extra symbol. This symbol is known as the 'facet indicator'.

Example : The digit 20 has several shades of meaning in the tables. But the addition of an extra symbol (or facet indicator) determines the facet i.e.

(20) means ecosphere,

"20" means twenty-first century A.D.

= 20 signifies language and so on.

The independent auxiliary tables are affixed to UDC numbers when needed and also used in isolation to form class numbers for documents. These are the auxiliaries of language, form, place, race and time. These tables have biterminal signs, i.e. signs that enclose the number and demarcate it from adjacent ones. These biterminal signs enable the auxiliaries to be affixed anywhere within a UDC number with a few exceptions.

The dependent auxiliary tables are not used in isolation but are always affixed to UDC numbers.

The special auxiliaries denote those characteristics which are recurrent locally. These are different from common auxiliaries and can be applied to a limited range of main tables. Special auxiliaries are dispersed throughout the table and are of limited applicability and are denoted by notation.

Structure of UDC

The structure of UDC in the form of upturned tree, can be represented as under :

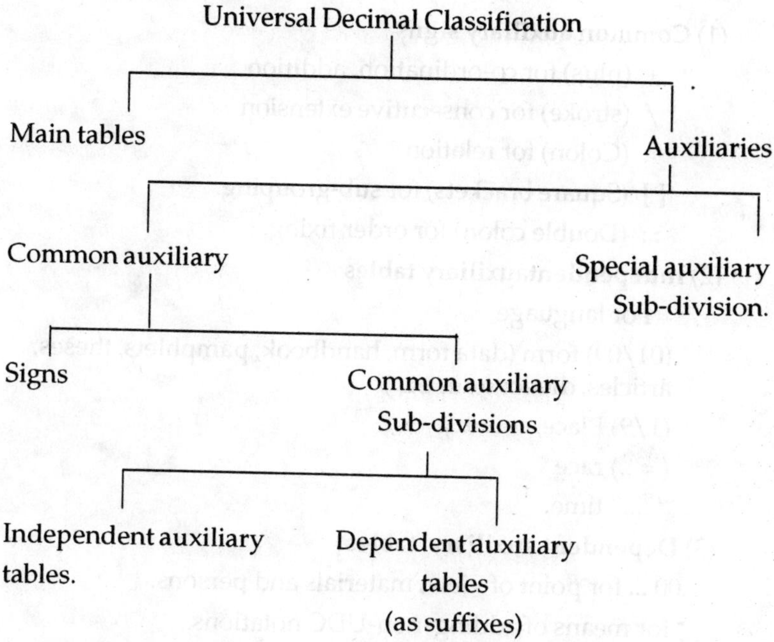

Difference between DDC and UDC

The main difference between the DDC and UDC is that the classes in the former are made up of three digits, while in the latter it is one. The DDC has three auxiliary tables and the auxiliaries are many with multiple uses and approaches. The fifth edition of the DDC has formed the basis on which the UDC had been built. The division of classes in both the classification schemes remains almost the same. In spite of the narrow base, the ingenious feature of the DDC is that the decimal system allows the classes to be divided and sub-divided to any extent. The UDC numbers can be formulated for all subjects compound or complex due to the fact that UDC has decimal system with the provision of connective symbols, with common and special auxiliaries.

Auxiliary Signs and Tables

The following are the auxiliary signs, independent and dependent tables followed by auxiliary sub-divisions.

(1) Common auxiliary signs

+ (plus) for co-ordination, addition

/ (stroke) for consecutive extension

: (Colon) for relation

[ ] (Square brackets) for sub-grouping.

: : (Double colon) for order fixing.

(2) Independentauxiliary tables

= For language

(01/09) form (data form, handbook, pamphlets, theses, articles, dictionaries etc.)

(1/9) Place, country.

(= ..) race

" ...." time.

(3) Dependent auxiliary tables

.00 ... for point of view, materials and persons.

* for means of adding non-UDC notations.

These auxiliaries form the vital connecting link between different facets of compound and complex numbers.

(4) Special auxiliary sub-divisions

These sub-divisions which introduce recurring concepts, are denoted as under :

- 1/-9 Hyphen series	Not of much relevance to forestry
.01/.09 point - nought series	
'1/' 9 Apostrophe series	

- -01/- -09 (double hyphen series) - Subject numbers -

The double hyphen is peculiar to the oxford system of decimal classification.

It is used as an 'auxiliary number' having a sense more specific than the true auxiliaries. It is used to denote special auxiliary subject numbers - - 01/- -09. In filing under the key number to which it is appended, it has the same function as the colon.

Now the details of individual signs and sub-divisions are shown as below :

Common Auxiliary Signs

(i)Symbol + (plus) for coordination, addition

When a compound subject can not be denoted by a single number this symbol connects (or coordinates) two or more separated non-consecutive UDC numbers to signify the concept e.g.

452 + 453 Birds and Insects

(540 + 549) India and Pakistan (note the bracket)

847 + 854 Drying and grading of converted timber

(ii) Symbol / (stroke) for consecutive extension.

When no number exists for a compound subject comprising a range of concepts, it can be denoted by the extension sign which connects two or more separated (non-consecutive) UDC numbers, e.g.

382 / 383 Buildings, Roads and Bridges.

321 / 327 Marking, Felling inventory.

847 / 848 Drying, handling and storage of timber.

(iii) Symbol : (colon) for relation.

A general, coordinating and reversible relation is indicated where the concepts involved are of equal significance e.g.

31 : 78 Logging and Transport in relation to Economics.

2 : 414 Economics in relation to Chemical Control.

74 (44 : 54) Forest Produce trade policy of France in relation to India.

74 (54 : 44) Forest produce trade policy of India in relation to France.

847 . 2 : (048 .1) and/or 847.2 (048.1) Bibliography on Kiln drying.

847 . 2 : (43) and /or 847.2 (43) Kiln drying in Germany.

(iv) Symbol [ ] (square brackets) for subgrouping.

When a compound number, denoted by two or more numbers are linked together by plus or colon, and the resultant number, in turn, is related to another number by colon (or modified by common or special auxiliary), this symbol is used for subgrouping the concepts e.g.

146 (540) : [05 . 014] Indian Vertebrates, surveys and classification.

Here 146 (54) Indian Vertebrates.

and [05.015] Surveys and classification.

(v) Symbol : : (double colon) for order fixing.

When the compound numbers in a compound subject is fixed by : : symbol, the arrangement becomes irreversible. This symbol is, therefore, useful in an UDC classified collection of computerised information retrieval system. In such case, the aforesaid subject will be denoted by the following number.

146 (54) : : [05] : 014 Indian Vertebrates, Surveys and classification.

Independent Auxiliary Tables

Symbol = (equal) denotes languages.

When a main UDC number expresses the subject of document, its linguistic form or language is denoted by these auxiliaries. It may be used when a very coextensive classification is needed for documents with emphasis on language or where detailed filing order is needed. This sign can be prefixed or suffixed.

If the document has to be filed by language, the sign is prefixed e.g.

= 44 (043. 811.4) Dissertation on growth rings in French language.

Where necessary, the auxiliary may be separated from the main number by colon e.g

= 43: 021.832.1 Handbook on sawmilling in German language.

The auxiliary is suffixed when the filing order is by subject, e.g.,

114 (038) = 51 technical dictionary on Soil science in Chinese language.

Form Auxiliaries

Symbol (01/09) (bracket nought) denotes form.

The form of presentation or documentary form of a subject represented by a main UDC number can be expressed by these auxiliaries e.g.

132 (031) Encyclopaedias on Plant Pathology.

When documents have to be arranged according to form, the auxiliary will be cited first e.g.

(042) 812.7 Lectures on strength properties.

Place Auxiliaries

Symbol (1/9) (brackets - one to nine) for denoting place.

When a subject is denoted by a main UDC number, its geographical area, locations or space are indicated by place auxiliaries e.g.

943 (410)	Forest Insurance in Great Britain.
841 (5)	Wood preservation in Asia

For creating a filing sequence based on place, the auxiliary may be placed first to create the following number :

(411) 832.3 Scotland — Match factories.

The place auxiliary may also be placed at the end e.g.

832.3 (411) Match factories in Scotland.

For classification of maps (where the emphasis is on place aspect), only place auxiliary can be used.

Race and Nationality Auxiliaries

Symbol (= ...) (brackets - equals) for denoting race, nationality etc.

The nationality or ethnic aspects of a subject (represented by a main UDC number) are denoted by these auxiliaries, e.g.

652 (= 47) Forest valuation by Russians.

Time Auxiliaries

Symbol "....." (double quotation marks) denotes time.

When a subject is represented by a main UDC number, its date, range or point of time can be denoted by these time auxiliaries, e.g.

64 "20" Forestry as business in twenty first Century AD

In addition to double quotation marks, plus and minus signs are also prefixed to distinguish the dates BC and AD e.g.

"— 0087" BC 87
"+ 0072" AD 72

Symbol—05 (hyphen nought five) for persons and their characteristics.

Sometimes a subject has personal aspects secondary to it and no direct sub-division or special auxiliary is available for denoting the concept. In such cases, the persons concerned or their characteristics are denoted by these auxiliary sub-division. This fact will be clear from examples showing different aspects of the problems.

The personal aspect of a subject can be expressed through the auxiliary -05 e.g.

2	Silviculture
2.05	Silviculturist

When the agent is supposed to be denoted by the auxiliary - 051 e.g.

0	Forestry:
0.051	Foresters.

Double hyphen (- -)

The double hyphen (- -) is peculiar to the present forestry classification. It has two closely related functions : (1) to denote the special auxiliary subject numbers - - 01 / - - 09, and (ii) to show when it precedes a main number, and is used as an "auxiliary number" having a sense more specific than the true auxiliaries. In filing under the key number to which it is appended, however it has the same function as the colon i.e.

174.7 - - 811 is treated exactly as if it were written 174.7 : 811.

The other examples of double hyphen (- -) are :

847.7 - - 01 Research on Kiln drying.

847.2 - - 090.2 History of Kiln drying.

847.2 : 174.7 and /or 847.2 - - 174.7 Kiln drying of conifers.

3

Oxford System of Decimal Classification

Introduction

The classification is the process whereby similar things are grouped together, while dissimilar ones are separated. This principle can be extended to ideas contained in document. When this is done there emerges the field of library or document classification. Things which do not have the common feature are excluded. When the things have some common features they can be grouped into a class. This class can, in turn, be divided into smaller classes on the basis of common distinctiveness. The process is continued until the entire gamut from the universe of knowledge to a class with only one number is theoretically covered. All useful classes containing groups of related things, lie between these two extreme ends.

Melvil Dewey was the originator of the system. The Dewey system encompasses all recorded knowledge into ten main classes. These main classes are numbered from 0-9. Each of these main classes, in turn are divided into ten divisions and then each of these divisions into ten sections. The notation in its simplest form consists of three digits. But numbers derived through multiple synthesis for denoting specific topics could be very long.

Classification

The following are the principles of decimal classification :

(a) The decimal point

This system of decimal classification rests upon the assumption that all of the sub-divisions given are preceded by the decimal point, i.e. are represented as decimal fractions of some number which signifies the whole of knowledge in the subject concerned. Thus in the present system the ten primary heads if expressed in full would be .0 (Forests, forestry and the utilization of forest products) to .9 (Forests and forestry from the national point of view—social economics of forestry) and every sub-division of heads would be similarly preceded by the decimal point. By convention this point is omitted in writing. Before filing it is important to remember its existence if we are to understand why e.g. (.) 239 precedes (.) 24.

(b) Meaning of .0 and .9

It is extremely important in cataloguing that the general heads should not be mixed with the particular heads. If this mistake happens the important references are apt to be buried in the number card. This is taken care of by providing the digit 0.9 (remembering that the decimal point will actually be written only after each group of 3 figures). Precisely defined 0.9 means "Miscellaneous topics belonging to the head of next rank but not classified at any of its sub-divisions .0 to .8'. The number 819 thus signifies "Any property that which can not be classified under any of the heads 810-818". The use of .9 appears to be the only satisfactory means of guaranteeing accommodation within the decimal scale for rare or new topics of next higher rank, and if such topics become sufficiently numerous or important, the way is open for use of the digits .91/.98 in which case 0.99 becomes new "miscellaneous" head.

At the other end of the decimal scale .0 of any number has been left open, so far as possible for eventual sub-divisions of more general import than the heads 0.1/.9. It is to be noted that .0 is not identical with the head of which it is the first subdivision e.g. 114.3 and 114.30 are seen from their titles to differ, in fact the latter having a more restricted meaning.

(c) Occasional Deviations from Strict Decimal Subordination

In principle, subdivisions of a given subject ought to receive numbers decimally subordinate to the number for that subject. This, however is an ideal that should not be pressed too far because there is no natural connection that exists between the conventional sub-divisions of knowledge and the available digits of the decimal scale nor any absolute relation between the length of a decimal number and the "importance" of the subject that it denotes. Practical considerations invite and justify departures from strict decimal ranking in special cases.

In this text the detailed and exhaustive sub-divisions have not been recommended because the libraries in the office of the Conservator of Forests and Dy. C. F. etc. will not contain books more than 5000 to 10,000. Moreover the untrained staff working in the library may do mistakes and blunders while giving a number to the book.

(d) Main and Auxiliary numbers, Simple and Compound Numbers

The decimal numbers of the subject classification proper are called *main numbers.* Any main number standing alone, with no further symbols or numbers is a *simple number* and it is clear that simple numbers give no special problems of filing order.

The oxford system also provides auxiliary numbers of three kinds for the finer classification of references: (i) auxiliary numbers of subject; (ii) auxiliary numbers of form; and (iii) auxiliary numbers of place, or geographical numbers.

In order to combine the ideas a main number may be combined, using standard connecting symbols, denoting the type of combination, with some other main number(s), auxiliary number(s) or both. The result is termed a *compound number* and again according to the connecting symbols used some or all of its component parts may be given separate cards in the catalogue i.e. the ideas may be *cross referenced.* The first component in such a case may be called the *key number.*

(e) Alphabetical index

This should be compiled to facilitate the use of the system. It should also assist those who wish to construct a concordance with any other system. Users should not rely on this index alone, but should consult the number in the context of the system.

CLASSIFICATION SCHEDULE OF ODC

(Subject Classification- Conspectus of Primary Heads)

0 Forests, forestry and the utilization of forest products.
1. Factors of the environment, Biology.
2. Silviculture
3. Work science (Work studies). Harvesting of wood : logging and transport. Forest Engineering.
4. Forest injuries and protection.
5. Forest mensuration. Increment; development and structure of stands. Surveying and mapping.
6. Forest management, Business economics of forestry. Administration and organization of Forest Enterprises.
7. Marketing of forest products. Economics of forest transport and the wood industries.
8. Forest products and their utilization.
9. Forests and forestry from the national point of view. Social economics of forestry.

- - 01 / - -09 Auxiliary subject numbers

(0) - Auxiliary numbers of form

(1/9) Auxiliary numbers of place

---

0. FORESTS, FORESTRY AND THE UTILIZATION OF FOREST PRODUCTS

The cipher 0 is the most general head of the scheme; it must on no account be subdivided expect by means of auxiliary numbers or cross-references *i.e.* the heads 01/09 are prohibited, but combinations such as 0 - - 011 (= forest terminology) and 0 (031) (= encyclopaedia of forestry) are allowed.

I. **FACTORS OF THE ENVIRONMENT BIOLOGY.** (Conspectus of Primary Subheads)

11. Site factors : Climate, situation, soil, hydrology (Water conservation, soil conservation and erosion).
12. General biology
13. General Zoology

14. Systematic Zoology
15. Animal ecology, Game and fish management, hunting, shooting and fishing.
16. General botany,
17. Systematic botany
18. Plant ecology
19. Miscellaneous

---

11. SITE FACTORS : CLIMATE, SITUATION, SOIL HYDROLOGY (WATER CONSERVATION, SOIL CONSERVATION AND EROSION)

111 The atmosphere, Meteorology. Climate and microclimate.

111.0 Practical meteorology (methods, data, forecasts, etc).

111.1 Composition, structure, mechanics and thermodynamics of the atmosphere in general.

111.2 Radiation and temperature (Radiation, Solar, Air temperature etc.)

111.4 Atmospheric pressure

111.5 Wind

111.7 Humidity, evaporation, Clouds etc. Precipitation.

111.8 Climatology (Solar climate, climatic changes, microclimate, environment etc.)

111.9 Various influences and phenomena (Cosmic, optical, Electrical, Acoustic).

113 Situation (longitude, latitude, altitude, topography etc.)

114 Soil. Soil science

114.1 Soil physics (All physical properties of soil)

114.2 Soil Chemistry (Arranged in parallel with UDC 631.41 (Colloidal properties, Absorption, soil reaction, pH value, soil solution etc.)

114.3 Soil formation. The soil profile and its development. (litter and humus layers etc.)

114.4 Soil classification, Soil types.

114.41 General matters

114.44 Genetic classification of soil types.

114.46 Traditional (mainly textural) soil classification.

114.49 Miscellaneous

114.5 Soil fertility. Soil toxicity

114.6 Soil biology (Arranged in parallel with UDC 631.46).

114.7 Soil surveys and surveying

114.9 Miscellaneous

116 Hydrology. Water conservation, soil conservation and erosion.

116.1 Studies of the effects of vegetation of precipitation. Evaporation (including transpiration) and atmospheric humidity etc. (Canopy interception of rain; drip, precipitation etc.)

116.2 Studies of infiltration, run-off and water erosion.

116.3 Special studies of stream-flow and bank erosion

116.4 Special studies of Wind erosion

116.5 Erosion along roads, railways and canals

116.6 General accounts of erosion and practical erosion control. (Control on pasture land, contouring, farm cropping etc.)

116.7 Special measures for the correction and maintenance of water channels

116.8 Coast erosion and protection. Special measures for sand fixation (on the coast or inland).

116.9 Miscellaneous

12 GENERAL BIOLOGY (Chiefly for Library Classification of Books).

13 GENERAL ZOOLOGY

130 Animal Biochemistry

131 Physiology (Blood circulation, Respiration, nutrition, nervous system etc.)

132 Pathology. Teratology. Deformities

133 Embryology. Ontogeny

134 Organology. Anatomy (Circulatory system, Respiratory system etc.)

135 Phylogeny, evolution. Heredity, genetics and breeding, Variation.

136 Economic Zoology (general)

136.1 Useful animals

136.5 Harmful animals

138 Histology

139 Miscellaneous

14 SYSTEMATIC ZOOLOGY

142 Invertebrata

146 Vertebrata

15 ANIMAL ECOLOGY, GAME AND FISH MANAGEMENT, HUNTING, SHOOTING AND FISHING

151 Mode of life, autecology, habits, adaptability.

152 Animal sociology, animal communities

153 Fluctuations and cycles of population

156 Game management. Hunting and shooting

157 Fish management. Fishing.

159 Miscellaneous

16 GENERAL BOTANY

160 Plant Chemistry (Chemical composition, Elements and compounds, essential and non-essential, stimulants etc.)

161 Physiology (circulation of water and gases, Absorption Exudation, Transpiration, Assimilation, Photosynthesis, cell physiology etc.)

162 Pathology and teratology.

163 Embryology

164 Morphology (organs of lower plants, roots, stems, leaves flowers, seeds etc.)

165 Phylogeny, evolution, Heredity, genetics and breeding, Variation.

166 Economic botany (general) (useful plants and harmful plants)

168 Histology

169 Miscellaneous

17 SYSTEMATIC BOTANY

170.1 Herbaria

172.1 Cryptograms (Algae, Lichens, Bryophyta etc.)

174 Embryophyta. Simphonogamia, Spermatophyta. Phanero gams. Seed-plants in general. (coniferae, Angiospermae, mono-cot, Dicot etc.)

18 PLANT ECOLOGY

181 Mode of life, autecology, Silvicultural characters of trees.

181.1 Distribution, natural range.

181.2 Atmospheric relations. Acclimatization

181.3 Water, soil and root relations.

181.4 Reaction to biotic influences and fire. (Plant competition etc.)

181.5 Reproductive behavior (Asexual, Sexual, Pollination, fruiting, seed dispersal, longevity, dormancy, germination, seedling development etc.)

181.6 Life form, habit, Post-seedling development and form. (Crown form, self pruning, stem form etc.)

181.7 Duration, longevity, stature, records of exceptional age or size. Effects of age on behavior.

181.8 Phenology

181.9 Miscellaneous

182 Synecology, Plant sociology (general, principles and methods).

182.1 Palaeoecology, History of vegetation.

182.2 Succession, alternation and periodicity in vegetation (Seral communities, climaxes and preclimaxes, seasonal aspects etc.)

182.3 Units of vegetation (associations etc.)

182.4 Layer Communities (Dominant tree, understorey, ground layers, shrubs, etc.)

182.5 Synecological measurements and methods

182.8 Ecology of artificial (cultivated) plant communities etc.

182.9 Miscellaneous

187 Vegetation types

189 Miscellaneous

19 MISCELLANEOUS

---

2 SILVICULTURE (Conspectus of Primary Sub-heads)

22 Silvicultural systems. Constitution and composition of stands; forms of stand

23 Regeneration and formation of stands

24 Tending of stands and trees

25 Treatment of defective, derelict or very open stands

26 Combinations of forestry with agricultural and pastoral husbandry (including shelterbelts & their treatment)

27 Arboreta. Arboriculture for ornamental purposes. Hedges and hedge plants

28 Husbandry of forest products other than wood

29 Miscellaneous

---

22 SILVICULTURAL SYSTEMS. CONSTITUTION AND COMPOSITION OF STANDS : FORMS OF STAND.

221. High forest systems (clear felling, shelterwood felling, selection felling etc.)

221.23 Group system. Irregular shelterwood system. *Femelschlag* (Swiss etc.)

221.5 Accessory systems (High forests with reserves, Two storeyed forests etc.)

222 Coppice, pollarding and lopping systems

226 Changes of Silvicultural system. Conversion (by system or species)

228 Constitution and composition of stands; forms of stand. (choice of species, Dominance and suppression, pure and mixed stands, artificial and natural stands)

228.7 Artificial stands, plantations

228.8 Natural stands

23 REGENERATION AND FORMATION OF STANDS

230 Forms of regeneration (over large areas, by groups by strips etc.)

231 Natural regeneration (advance growth, canopy manipulation, ground vegetation etc.)

232 Artificial regeneration

232.1 Choice and trial of species, races etc., (provenance trials etc.)

232.2 Preparatory work, auxiliary measures (site preparation, burning, soil preparation, Irrigation etc.)

232.3 Seed, nursery practice, direct sowing

232.31 Seed (Plus trees, elite trees, seed orchards or, seed collection, storage, pretreatment etc.)

232.32 Plant rearing. Nursery practice

232.321 Nursery sites, including factors affecting selection of sites for nurseries.

232.322 Preparation and treatment of soil, including maintenance of fertility. (Inorganic fertilizers, organic manures, compost etc.)

232.323 Sowing and covering.

232.324 Transplanting and lining out

232.325 Tending (in both seedbeds and transplant beds)—(watering, weedings, weed killers, mulching, Thinning out etc.)

232.326 Salvage of overgrown seedlings and transplants. Root or shoot pruning etc. (root shoot pruning, undercutting etc.)

232.327 Protection measures in nurseries. (from wind, rain, fungus etc.)

232.328 Vegetative propagation

232.329 Miscellaneous (Green houses, heated frames, cold frames etc.)

232.33 Formation of stands by direct sowing

232.4 Formation of stands by planting

232.41 Planting stock (age, grading, root pruning, heeling—in etc.)

232.42 Methods of planting. Fertilizers etc. (Pitting, mounding etc.)

232.43 Spacing and arrangement in plantations

232.44 Season and time of planting

232.49 Miscellaneous

232.5 Artificial formation of stands by vegetative propagation (e.g. direct planting of unrooted cuttings)

233 Afforestation (of particular types of land).

234 Formation of forest by natural succession.

235 Underplanting, advance planting etc. Nurses and formation of mixtures.

236 Care of regeneration or plantations in the initial stages of establishment.

237 Amelioration of forest sites.

238 Timber plantation crops requiring special treatment (e.g. Poplar plantations, rootwood of Erica arborea etc.)

239 Miscellaneous.

24 TENDING OF STANDS AND TREES

241 Cleanings

242 Thinnings

243 Opening of the Canopy (increment fellings, overhead release and improvement fellings).

244 Climber cutting etc.

245 Tending of trees

249 Miscellaneous

25 TREATMENT OF DEFECTIVE, DERELICT OR VERY OPEN STANDS

26 COMBINATIONS OF FORESTRY WITH AGRICULTURE AND PASTORAL HUSBANDRY (INCLUDING SHELTERBELTS AND THEIR TREATMENT).

261 Alternate forestry and Agriculture, periodic or temporary agricultural use of forest land

262 Fuel and fodder forests

263 Irrigated forests

264 Farm forests

265 Strips of lines at road, rail and canal sides etc., hedgerow trees

266 Shelterbelts, windbreaks.

268 Pastured forests, Grazing on forests and open ranges.

269 Miscellaneous

27 ARBORETA, ARBORICULTURE FOR ORNAMENTAL PURPOSES, HEDGES AND

28 HUSBANDRY (GROWING AND COLLECTION) OF FOREST PRODUCTS OTHER THAN WOOD.

281 Christmas trees

282 Bark crops

283 Fruit and Seed crops

284 Crops tapped for exudations

285 Leaf crops.

286 Osier-growing

287 Bamboo - and Cane-growing.

288 Crops grown for animal products (e.g. lac, silkworms).

289 Miscellaneous

29 MISCELLANEOUS

---

3. WORK SCIENCE (WORK STUDIES), HARVESTING OF WOOD, LOGGING AND TRANSPORT. FOREST ENGINEERING. (Conspectus of primary sub-heads)

30 Work science (Work studies) : general

31 Logging and transport : general

32 Felling and related operations

33 Degree of utilization and waste. Clearing the felling site

34 Storage of wood in the forest and at log dumps (landings)

35 Performance measurements for determining piece rates in felling and related operations.

36 Tools, machines and equipment for felling and related operations

37 Transport

38 Forest Engineering

39 Miscellaneous.

---

30 WORK SCIENCE (WORK STUDIES) : GENERAL

31 LOGGING AND TRANSPORT : GENERAL

32 FELLING AND RELATED OPERATIONS

321 Marking

322 Preparatory measures other than marking. Felling season.

323 Felling and subsequent primary conversion

324 Stacking

325 Sorting and assortments of wood in the rough.

326 Sequence of operations

327 Inventory and control of fellings and of work in felling and related operations.

329 Miscellaneous.

33 DEGREE OF UTILIZATION AND WASTE, CLEARING THE FELLING SITE.

331 Degree of utilization and waste : General.

332 Clearing the felling site. (Relogging, slash disposal, etc.)

333 Harvesting of small wood (e.g. from tending operations)

339 Miscellaneous

34 STORAGE OF WOOD IN THE FOREST AND AT LOG DUMPS ("LANDINGS")

35 PERFORMANCE MEASUREMENTS FOR DETERMINING PIECE RATES IN FELLING RELATED OPERATIONS. ("LANDINGS")

36 TOOLS, MACHINES AND EQUIPMENT FOR FELLING AND RELATED OPERATIONS.

361 Barking tools and machines

362 Sawing tools and machines

363 Tools & Machines for cutting (hewing) & cleaving (Axes, billbooks, Knives, wedges, cleaving hammers, machines etc.)

364 Tools and equipment for handling wood (hooks, Pickaroons, jacks etc.)

365 Measuring and marking tools and equipment

367 Stump-grubbing tools and equipment.

369 Miscellaneous (e.g. faggot-binders, ladders, climbing equipment).

37 TRANSPORT

371 Loading and unloading.

372 Land and air transport: General (Slides, sledgeways, by man and animals, cable methods, winches by tractor, lorry, railway etc.)

377 Equipment for loading and unloading, skidding and hauling (loading and unloading equipments, cables, winches, engines, hand tools etc.)

378 Water transport

379 Miscellaneous

38 FOREST ENGINEERING

381 Materials (Explosives and constructional materials etc.)

382 Buildings (logging camps, staff and labour quarters etc.)

383 Roads and bridges.

384 Protective Works (against erosion, landslip etc.)

385 Drainage, irrigation, sedimentation, water supply.

386 Waterways, stream training. (Engineering aspects).

387 Telephonic communications etc.

389 Miscellaneous

39 MISCELLANEOUS

---

4 FOREST INJURIES AND PROTECTION

(conspectus of Primary sub-heads)

41 General Technique of Forest protection. Types of injury.

42 Injuries from inorganic agencies (excluding fire)

43 Forest Fires

44 Damage by harmful plants. Virus diseases

45 Damage by animals

46 Damage to tree growth by man

48 Injuries due to unknown or complex causes (arranged by tree species).

49 Miscellaneous

---

41 GENERAL TECHNIQUE OF FOREST PROTECTION. TYPES OF INJURY.

411 Natural and biological Control

412 Silvicultural control

413 Physical and Mechanical Control (Trapping shooting, removal of plant etc.)

414 Chemical Control (Poison baits, repellants, spraying, fumigation etc.)

415 Other means of Control

416 Types of injury (Defoliation, curls, spots, wilts, etc; to-bark, wood etc.)

419 Miscellaneous

42 INJURIES FROM INORGANIC AGENCIES (EXCLUDING FIRE)

421 Air currents (storms, constant winds)

422 Temperature influences. Insolation (Frost, heat, Sun-scorch, Drought etc.)

423 Precipitations (Rain, snow, Avalanches, frost etc.)

424 Soil conditions; erosion effects

425 Chemical influences (atmospheric—Gases and suspended matter etc.)

426 Electrical and cosmic influences

429 Miscellaneous

43 FOREST FIRES

431 Predisposing factors and causes. Fire danger. Fire behavior.

432 Prevention and Control

432.0 General preparedness and organization (Presuppression, general).

432.1 Advance measures (to prevent fires, reduce fire danger or restrict fire spread).

432.2 Detection and reporting (Ground patrols, Aerial observations etc.)

432.3 Suppression (Methods of suppression, fire lines, counter firing etc.)

432.9 Miscellaneous

433 Salvage and disposal of fire-damaged timber.

434 Revegetation etc. of burnt areas.
435 Benefits of fire control. Injurious effects of fire.
436 Beneficial effects of fire. Uses of fire in silviculture and other forms of husbandry.
439 Miscellaneous
44 DAMAGE BY HARMFUL PLANTS, VIRUS DISEASES.
441 Forest Weeds
442 Parasitic (Higher) plants. Climbers and epiphytes.
443 Fungi and bacteria.
444 Virus diseases
449 Miscellaneous
45 DAMAGE BY ANIMALS
451 Mammals
452 Birds
453 Insects
459 Other animals
46 DAMAGE TO TREE GROWTH BY MAN
48 INJURIES DUE TO UNKNOWN OR COMPLEX CAUSES (ARRANGED BY TREE SPECIES).
49 Miscellaneous

---

5 FOREST MENSURATION. INCREMENT; DEVELOPMENT AND STRUCTURE OF STANDS. SURVEYING AND MAPPING.

(Conspectus of Primary subheads.)

51 Systems and units of measurement (including conversions tables)
52 Measurements of the stem dimensions and volume of trees stands, forests and timber
53 Special measurements of trees and stands (Crown dimensions, stand density etc.)
54 Assessment of site quality.
55 Age determination
56 Increment; Development & structure of stands.
58 Surveying and Mapping. Aerial survey.
59 Miscellaneous

---

51 SYSTEMS AND UNITS OF MEASUREMENT (INCLUDING CONVERSION TABLES)

511 Metric system : General

512 British and American systems : General

513 Other systems : General

514 Linear and area measures

516 Solid volume

517 Stacked Volume.

518 Weight

519 Miscellaneous

52 MEASUREMENTS OF THE STEM DIMENSIONS AND VOLUME OF TREES, STANDS, FORESTS AND TIMBER.

521 Diameter (Girth) and sectional area

522 Height, length

523 Bark (including bark increment)

524 Determination of the volume of trees and stands.

524.1 Principles of volume determination. Form (Taper).

524.2 Volume of Single trees

524.3 Volume of tree groups and stands (e.g. sample plots)

524.4 Recording of data. Organization of measuring parties and their work.

524.6 General Surveys of forests and tracts of forest. Partial enumeration surveys, timber cruising

524.9 Miscellaneous

525 Volume by assortments. Merchantable Volume

526 Log measurement. "Scaling"

527 Solid volume of stacked products (including converting factors).

529 Miscellaneous

53 SPECIAL MEASUREMENTS OF TREES AND STANDS (CROWN DIMENSIONS, STAND DENSITY ETC.)

54 ASSESSMENT OF SITE QUALITY

55 AGE DETERMINATION

56 INCREMENT; DEVELOPMENT AND STRUCTURE OF STANDS

561 Increment in height, diameter, basal area, form and quality.

562 Volume increment

563 Increment determination in species having irregular or no growth rings.

564 Forecasting increment

565 Sample-plot technique

565 Yield tables and their construction.

567 Stand tables

568 Other mensurational studies of stand constitution and changes therein. Distribution of growth by classes etc.

569 Miscellaneous

58 SURVEYING AND MAPPING. AERIAL SURVEY

581/584 Grond surveys

585 Aerial reconnaissance and survey : General

589 Miscellaneous

59 MISCELLANEOUS

---

6. FOREST MANAGEMENT. BUSINESS ECONOMICS OF FORESTRY, ADMINISTRATION AND ORGANIZATION OF FOREST ENTERPRISES (Conspectus of Primary Subheads)

61 Forest Management : General, theory and principles

62 Methods of Management. Working plans. Annual or periodic yield. Yield regulation.

63 Other forest management questions

64 Forestry as a business : General

65 Special business problems of timber growing

66 Costing of logging operations

67 Assessment of financial results; book keeping and accountancy, business statistics; short-term planning and financing of forest enterprises

68 Administration and organization of forest enterprises

69 Miscellaneous.

---

61 FOREST MANAGEMENT : GENERAL, THEORY AND PRINCIPLES

62 METHODS OF MANAGEMENT, WORKING PLANS, ANNUAL OR PERIODIC YIELD, YIELD REGULATION.

63 OTHER FOREST MANAGEMENT QUESTIONS (For forest surveying and mapping)

64 FORESTRY AS A BUSINESS : GENERAL

65 SPECIAL BUSINESS PROBLEMS OF TIMBER-GROWING.

651 Calculation of Costs and profitability

652 Forest valuation

653 Value increment of the stem; development and structure of the stand as regards value

654 Determination of the objects of business management.

659 Miscellaneous

66 COSTING OF LOGGING OPERATIONS

661 Theory and Methods, costs and returns

662 Costs of different phases of work (cost items)

663 Different kinds of cost

664 Costs of particular assortments of wood

665 Influence of stem and log size on costs

666 Influence of particular forms of management and Silvicultural systems on costs

667 Budgeting and reviewing of costs

669 Miscellaneous

67 ASSESSMENT OF FINANCIAL RESULTS; BOOK-KEEPING AND ACCOUNTANCY; BUSINESS STATISTICS; SHORT-TERM PLANNING AND FINANCING.

671 Income, returns; expenditure, outlay; surplus, profit; Costs of permanent administrative arrangements

672 Assessment of financial results; balancing

673 Book keeping

674 Business statistics

676 Financing

677 Short-term planning and budgeting

679 Miscellaneous

68 ADMINISTRATION AND ORGANIZATION OF FOREST ENTERPRISES.

681 National (federal, State) forest services and administration

682 Private forest administration. Staff questions in private forestry.

683 Office organization

684 Labour management

685 Planning and organization of telecommunications.

686 Planning and organization of buildings, transport installations (roads etc.).

687 Planning and organization of the transport of men, supplies and equipment

689 Miscellaneous

69 MISCELLANEOUS

---

7. **MARKETING OF FOREST PRODUCTS. ECONOMICS OF FOREST TRANSPORT AND THE WOOD INDUSTRIES. (Conspectus of Primary Subheads)**

71 Marketing of forest products : General

72 The quantitative aspect of marketing; demand and supply.

73 Prices

74 Trade policy (other than trade customs and usages)

75 Trade customs and usages

76 Accountancy, business planning and administration in marketing.

77 Marketing : Miscellaneous

78 Economics of forest transport

79 Economics of the forest products industries.

---

71 MARKETING OF FOREST PRODUCTS : GENERAL

72 THE QUANTITATIVE ASPECTS OF MARKETING; DEMAND AND SUPPLY

721 Domestic Markets

722 International markets.

73 PRICES

74 TRADE POLICY (OTHER THAN TRADE CUSTOMS AND USAGES)

741 Domestic

742 International

75 TRADE CUSTOMS AND USAGES

76 ACCOUNTANCY, BUSINESS PLANNING AND ADMINISTRATION IN MARKETING.

77 MARKETING : MISCELLANEOUS

78 ECONOMICS OF FOREST TRANSPORT.

781 General

782 Quantities transported, their variations and trends

783 Tariffs, freights

784 Transport policy and other aspects of social economics in transport

785 Business practices and usages in transport

786 Accountancy, business planning and administration of transport.

788 Ports, harbours

789 Miscellaneous

79 ECONOMICS OF THE FOREST PRODUCTS INDUSTRIES

791 General

792 Output of the forest products industries; its variations and trends.

794 Industrial policy and other aspects of social economics in the forest products industries (except those in 792)

796 Accountancy, business planning and administration in the forest products industries.

799 Miscellaneous

---

8. FOREST PRODUCTS AND THEIR UTILIZATION (Conspectus of Primary Subheads)

81 Wood and bark : Structure and properties

82 Conversion, shaping, assembly and finishing of wood : General.

83. Timber manufacturing industries and products. Uses of wood as such.
84 Preservative and other treatments to improve the properties of wood. Damage by biological agencies and its control. Seasoning. Timber-yard practice
85 Grading of wood and wood products
86 Pulp industries. Composite materials made wholly or partly of woody matter. Chemical utilization of wood.
88 Economy in the use of wood. Replacement of wood by competitive materials.
89 Minor forest products

---

81. WOOD AND BARK : STRUCTURE AND PROPERTIES.
810 General Information on woods.
811 Structure. Identification
811.1 Anatomical elements and tissues
811.2 Special features and abnormal structure (Anatomical aspects)
811.4 Growth rings.
811.5 Sapwood and heartwood
811.6 Texture, grain, figure.
811.7 Phloem; bark
811.9 Miscellaneous
812 Physical and mechanical properties.
812.1 Optical, acoustic, frictional, thermal and electrical properties.
812.2 Behavior with liquids and gases
812.3 Density : Specific gravity. Buoyancy
812.7 Strength properties : General
812.8 Workability, Working properties.
812.9 Miscellaneous
813 Wood chemistry
814 Natural durability, Old wood, Fossilized wood
815 Effect of growth factors on structure and properties.
819 Miscellaneous

82 CONVERSION, SHAPING, ASSEMBLY AND FINISHING OF WOOD GENERAL.

821 Barking

822 Saws and sawing (description and investigations of individual machines and their functions) bow saw, cirular saw, band saw etc.)

823 Planing, cutting of mouldings. Chiselling, mortising and tenoning. Boring. Turning

824 Forms of Joint. Jointing and assembly.

825 Cleaving. Adzing. Mechanical comminution

826 Peeling, Slicing, Trimming and edging of thin sheets.

827 Bending, Moulding (other than by cutting)

828 General carpentry and joinery.

829 Miscellaneous

829.1 Finishing (Colouring, sanding, surface filling, polishing, Varnishing etc.)

829.9 Miscellaneous

83 TIMBER MANUFACTURING INDUSTRIES AND PRODUCTS, USES OF WOOD AS SUCH

831 Fuelwood and various types of rough timber, (poles, posts, sleepers etc.)

832 Mills, their functions and products

832.1 Sawmills and planing mills.

832.2 Veneer and plywood mills, including the manufacture of composite-wood assemblies.

832.3 Match factories

832.4 Wooden-house factories

832.8 Integrated mills and combinations of mills.

832.9 Miscellaneous

833 Timber in buildings and engineering structures.

834 Shingles, cooperage, packing containers, baskets etc.

835 Industrial and domestic (utility) woodware, toys and models, sports and recreational goods, musical instruments, scientific and mathematical instruments, surgical applications etc. (Manufacture & Use)

836 Furniture and Cabinet-making. Ecclesiastical woodwork. Carving, Marquetry. Wooden ornaments

838 Vehicle manufacturing

839.1 Wood wool and its manufacture

839.2 Wood flour and its manufacture

839.8 Industrial waste wood, its processing and uses.

839.9 Miscellaneous

84 PRESERVATION AND OTHER TREATMENTS TO IMPROVE THE PROPERTIES OF WOOD. DAMAGE BY BIOLOGICAL AGENCIES AND ITS CONTROL SEASONING. TIMBERYARD PRACTICE (HANDLING AND STORAGE).

841 Wood preservation

842 Treatments to improve the resistance of wood to physical and chemical agencies.

843 Fireproofing and fire resistance

844 Attack by plant organisms

845 Attack by animals (borers, termites, control, biological control etc.)

846 Steaming

847 Drying (Seasoning)

848 Timberyard practice. Handling and storage of timber.

849 Miscellaneous

85 "GRADING" OF WOOD AND WOOD PRODUCTS.

851 Timber quality in general

852 Detection, recognition and assessment of injuries and defects.

853 Grading of wood in the rough

854 "Grading of converted timber.

859 Miscellaneous

86 PULP INDUSTRIES. COMPOSITE MATERIALS MADE WHOLLY OR PARTLY OF WOODY MATTER. CHEMICAL UTILIZATION OF WOOD.

861 Pulp and paper manufacture. Textile and other cellulose derivatives.

861.0 Raw materials etc. pulpwood and chips.
861.1 Pulping and pulp.
861.2 Papermaking : Paper and cardboard.
861.4 Manufacture of cellulose textiles (rayon, cellulose wool etc.)
861.5 Cellulose derivatives (Cellulose esters etc.)
861.6 Fodder cellulose
861.9 Miscellaneous
862 Composite materials made wholly or partly of woody matter.
863 Wood hydrolysis. Saccharification
864 Utilization of lignin.
865 Plastics
866 Utilization of wood extractives
867 Destructive distillation
88 ECOLOGY IN THE USE OF WOOD, REPLACEMENT OF WOOD BY COMPETITIVE MATERIALS.
89 OTHER ("MINOR") FOREST PRODUCTS.
891 Mineral products (including peat and coal)
892 Vegetable products
892.1 Grass, Litter, Leaf fodder
892.2 Agricultural products
892.3 Wood ashes
892.4 Bark Products. Tanstuffs. Cork.
892.5 Christmas trees. Ornamental trees and branches. Medicinal plants, Edible plants.
892.6 Resin and turpentine. Essential Oils. fixed Oils and fats. Waxes. Gums. Latex. Dyestuffs. Sap sugar.
892.7 Fruits. Seeds. Fibers, yarns and flosses.
892.8 Heather. Broom. Osiers. Canes and Bamboos.
892.9 Miscellaneous
893 Animal products (e.g. lac)
899 Miscellaneous.

9. FORESTS AND FORESTRY FROM THE NATIONAL POINT OF VIEW, SOCIAL ECONOMICS OF FORESTRY. (Conspectus of Primary Subheads)

90 General

91 Land use, land-use policy, Afforestation policy.

92 Forest ownership and ownership policy.

93 Public supervision and regulation of forestry, including legislation for these purposes.

94 Other methods to implement forest policy.

95 Forest taxation.

96 Forest labour questions; labour questions in wood transport and the wood industries.

97 International forest policy and other international Collaboration.

99 Miscellaneous

---

90 GENERAL

901 Theory, methods, systematics; peculiarities of forestry from the point of view of social economics.

902 History of forests and forestry

902.1 Biography. Obituary notices.

903 Forest policy, general : general systems, programmes Plans etc.

904 General regional accounts of forests and forestry.

905 Forest statistics and resources

906 Direct economic significance of forests (Position of forests and forestry in the national economy).

907 Indirect significance of forests (Rural amenity, National parks, home sanctuaries, Recreation etc.)

908 Relationship to other branches of husbandry and industry.

909 Miscellaneous.

91 LAND USE, LAND-USE OWNERSHIP POLICY, AFFORESTATION POLICY

92 FOREST OWNERSHIP AND OWNERSHIP POLICY.

93 PUBLIC SUPERVISION AND REGULATION OF FORESTRY, INCLUDING LEGISLATION FOR THESE PURPOSES.

94 OTHER METHODS TO IMPLEMENT FOREST POLICY.

941 State subsidies. Provision of land, seed, planting stock etc. free or at low cost.

942 Credits.

943 Forest insurance

944 Co-operation, Collaboration of forest owners.

945 Advisory services : Publicity, propaganda, education training, research.

946 Associations, societies, conferences, excursions, institutions.

949 Miscellaneous

95 FOREST TAXATION

96 FOREST LABOUR QUESTIONS; LABOUR QUESTION IN WOOD TRANSPORT AND THE WOOD INDUSTRIES.

97 INTERNATIONAL FOREST POLICY AND OTHER INTERNATIONAL COLLABORATION.

98 MISCELLANEOUS

Appendix–A

- -01/- -09 AUXILIARI SUBJECT NUMBERS (Conspectus of Primary Subheads.)

- -01 Research and testing. Experiments

- -02 Husbandry. Cultivation.

- -03 Harvesting. Collection of natural produce. Work technique and efficiency.

- -04 Protection

- -05 Surveys

- -06 Organisation and planning. Internal economics and finance. Administration.

- -07 Trade and Transport Economics.

- -08 Everyday operations, Production processes, products etc.

- -09 National, social and international aspects.

- -01 RESEARCH AND TESTING, EXPERIMENTS.
- -010 Technique and procedure in research and testing; general.
- -011 Terminology. Nomenclature
- -012 Culture and care of experimental organisms
- -013 Specimens (Samples)
- -014 Classification. Identification-Detection. Qualitative tests.
- -015 Measurements. Quantitative tests. Calculations. Statistical methods.
- -016 Microscopy (including the use of differential stains etc. for macroscopic identification)
- -017 Apparatus, instruments etc.
- -018 Results. Properties and behavior.
- -019 Miscellaneous
- -02 HUSBANDRY, CULTIVATION.
- -03 HARVESTING, COLLECTION OF NATURAL PRODUCE.
- -04 PROTECTION.
- -05 SURVEYS
- -06 ORGANIZATION AND PLANNING. INTERNAL ECONOMICS AND FINANCE, ADMINISTRATION.
- -07 TRADE AND TRANSPORT ECONOMICS
- -08 EVERYDAY OPERATIONS, PRODUCTION, PROCESSES, PRODUCTS ETC.
- -081 Materials, Fuel and power.
- -082 Preparatory operations.
- -083 Main phase of Operation.
- -084 Accessory and final operations.
- -086 Regulation of conditions during operations.
- -087 Apparatus, instruments, machinery.
- -88 Products and their uses.
- -09 NATIONAL, SOCIAL AND INTERNATIONAL ASPECTS.
- -090 General
- -092 Ownership

- -093	Public supervision and Control. Legislation.
- -094	Promotion of private enterprise.
- -095	Taxation
- -096	Labour policy
- -097	International activities.
- -099	Miscellaneous.

Appendix B

(0/9) AUXILIARY NUMBERS OF FORM AND PLACE

(The following is only a selection of the most useful numbers in this section of UDC, which should be consulted by any user requiring more detailed subdivisions)

(0)	AUXILIARY NUMBERS OF FORM
(02)	Systematically arranged data in book form.
(021)	Comprehensive works. Handbooks. Academic text books.
(023)	Books of limited scope. Elementary works. Popular manuals.
(03)	Alphabetically classified data in book form.
(031)	Encylopaedias and (descriptive) dictionaries of limited scope.
(038)	Language dictionaries. Technical dictionaries.
(041)	Brochures, Pamphlets, Reprints.
(042)	Lectures, addresses etc.
(043)	Theses, dissertations.
(044)	Letters, Correspondence. Circulars.
(045)	Articles in periodicals.
(046)	Newspaper articles.
(047)	Reports, Notices.
(047.1)	Progress reports.
(047.3)	Special reports.
(047.5)	Reports for the press. Press notices.
(047.6)	Press cuttings. Short notices.
(048.1)	Bibliographical lists (list of references, Reviews.)
(048.6)	Abridged editions.
(048.8)	Collected abstracts.

(05)	Periodicals, Documents published periodically.
(052/054)	Periodicals appearing more than once annually.
(058)	Annuals. Yearbooks.
(058.7)	Directories. Address books and list of addresses.
(059)	Almanacs. Calendars. Diaries.
(075)	School books. Educational Programmes.
(079.3)	Reports of expeditions and travels.
(079.5)	Questionnaires.
(081)	Collected works of individual authors.
(082)	Collected or Collective works of different authors.
(083.3)	Tables of mathematical formulae.
(083.4)	Statistical documents. Tables of statistics.
(083.5)	Numerical tables. Conversion tables. Ready reckoners.
(083.6)	Tabulated data other than numerical tables.
(083.7)	Standards. Specifications.
(083.8)	Lists. Inventories. Catalogues (for trade catalogues see (085).
(083.9)	Plans, Projects.
(084.11)	Drawings.
(084.121)	Photographs.
(084.122)	Cinema films.
(084.124)	Diapositives. Lantern slides etc.
(084.3)	Maps, plans.
(084.4)	Atlasses.
(084.5)	Pictorials, posters etc.
(085)	Publications of industrial and commercial undertakings, Catalogues. Prospectuses. Circulars. Advertisements etc.
(087.4)	Contracts, Agreements.
(088.7)	Factory and Trade marks.
(088.8)	Patents.

(1/9)	**AUXILIARY NUMBERS OF PLACE**
(1)	PLACE IN GENERAL

(100.2)	The whole world. All countries
(100.3)	Several countries or portions of the globe which do not together form an organic unit.
(2)	PHYSICAL LOCALITY
(212)	Temperate Zones
(213)	Subtropical and Tropical Zones.
(22)	Islands
(23)	Mountains
(25)	Plains
(26)	Oceans, Seas, At sea
(28)	Surface water, Fresh water
(4/9)	PLACES IN THE MODERN WORLD
(4)	EUROPE
(41)	Great Britain and Northern Ireland and British Commonwealth
(410)	United Kingdom of Great Britain and Northern Ireland.
(411)	Scotland
(415)	Ireland in General
(416)	Northern Ireland
(42)	England
(429)	Wales
(43)	Germany
(436)	Austria
(438)	Poland
(44)	France
(45)	Italy
(46)	Spain
(469)	Portugal
(47)	Russia; U.S.S.R.
(48)	Scandinavia
(481)	Norway
(485)	Sweden

(489)	Denmark
(491)	Iceland
(492)	The Netherlands (Holland)
(493)	Belgium
(494)	Switzerland
(495)	Greece
(496)	Turkey in Europe
(498)	Rumania
(5)	ASIA
(5-011)	The Near East
(5-012)	The Far East
(51)	China
(512.317)	Hong Kong
(515)	Tibet
(517)	Mongolia
(519)	Korea
(52)	Japan
(53)	Arabia
(54)	The sub continent of *India*
(540)	Republic of China
(548.7)	Ceylon
(549)	Pakistan
(55)	Persia Iran
(56)	Turkey in Asia, Asia Minor
(567)	Mesopotamia, Iraq
(57)	Siberia
(58)	Central Asia in General
(581)	Afghanistan
(591)	Burma
(591.9)	Andman and Nicobar Islands.
(593)	Siam, Thailand
(596/599)	Indo-China, French Indo-China
(6)	AFRICA
	All the countries of Africa

(7/8)	AMERICA IN GENERAL
(7)	NORTH AMERICA
(71)	Canada
(711)	British columbia
(72)	Mexico
(728)	Central America
(729)	West Indies
(73)	U.S.A.
(75)	South-east, South Atlantic States
(79)	Pacific States
(791)	Arizona
(794)	California
(798)	Alaska
(8)	SOUTH AMERICA
(803)	Latin America in General
(81)	Brazil
(82)	Argentina
(861)	Colombia
(862)	Panama
(87)	Venezuela
(88)	Guiana
(881)	British Guiana
(882)	French Guiana
(9)	OCEANIA
(91)	Malayan Archipelago Indonesia
(910)	Netherlands East Indies. Indonesian Republic
(911)	Borneo and Surounding Islands.
(914)	The Philippines
(921)	Sumatra
(922)	Java
(931)	New Zealand
(94)	Australia
(95)	New Guinea, Papua

(98/99) POLAR REGIONS

(98) Arctic Regions

(99) Antarctic regions.

Note :— List of all the Countries have not been given. Only important ones from the forestry point of view have been included.

Classes and Characteristics of O.D.C.

The decimal classification in being followed in about 75 per cent libraries of all types in India. But the Oxford system of decimal classification is hardly being adopted for the forest libraries. With the rapid increase in forestry books and literatures year after year, this is high time that each forest library should adopt the scientific management by using oxford system of decimal classification. The application requires lot of practice and experience.

In this chapter an effort has been made to introduce the use of various tables and auxiliaries in accordance with the O.D.C. It is quite probable that all the books in forestry may not find the exact place in the O.D.C. In such cases domestic sub-divisions may be used by the librarian.

Domestic Sub-division : Until sub-divisions are authorized any undivided main number may be sub-divided provided such sub-division remains entirely domestic and unofficial. Thus anyone is permitted to apply domestic sub-divisions to *325 (Sorting and assortment of wood in the rough) or 326 (sequence of operations including e.g. felling instructions, traditional order of operations, primary conversion after extraction etc.). Whereas in the former case, the number is marked with an asterisk, he may do so with safety as the asterisk denotes numbers for which it has been decided that no one method of sub-division could gain international acceptance. But he cannot take the vacant numbers of a partly sub-divided head and fill them domestically; these vacancies are reserved for any new heads that may from time to time be officially approved, e.g. by promotion from the miscellaneous head. .9. under 31 (Logging and Transport - general). for example, the only numbers that may be used are 311, 312 and 319, and if domestic sub-divisions are wanted they must be applied to one or other of these three heads, the heads 313/318 being left vacant. Further, when a number is domestically sub-divided the symbol × (cross) should be inserted between the approved head and its domestic sub-divisions, e.g., 319 x 1, 319 x 2 etc. This symbol does not affect the filing order, and if it coincides with the conventional decimal point—as in the above example—the latter is best omitted, 319 x 1 being read for filing as 319.1, while it is undesirable that domestic numbers should appear at all in printed literature, it is essential that, if they do so, they should be clearly designated as such—and thus the symbol × suitably provided for.

In the O.D.C. the following tables have been provided.

(1) Table 0 — Forests, forestry and the utilization of forest products.

(2) Table 1 — Factors of the Environment, Biology.

(3) Table 2 — Silviculture

(4) Table 3 — Work Science (work studies).
Harvesting of Wood : Logging and Transport, Forest Engineering.

(5) Table 4 — Forest injuries and Protection.

(6) Table 5 — Forest Mensuration. Increment, Development and Structure of stands. Surveying and mapping.

(7) Table 6 — Forest Management, Business Economics of forestry, Administration and organisation of forest enterprises.

(8) Table 7 — Marketing of forest Products. Economics of forest Transport and the wood industries.

(9) Table 8 — Forest Products and their utilization.

(10) Table 9 — Forests and Forestry from the National Point of view. Social Economics of forestry.

(11) Appendix A — i.e. --01/--09 Auxiliary Subject Numbers.

(12) Appendix B — (0/9) Auxiliary numbers of form and place.
(0) Auxiliary numbers of form.
(1/9) Auxiliary numbers of place.

(13) Appendix C — Alphabetical index to domestic sub-divisions of 145.7 (insecta), Alphabetical index I—of subjects and form numbers, Alphabetical index D—of Geographical numbers.

Note :—For an ordinary forest library the use of Appendix C—may be dispensed with as it is too comprehensive.

In order to understand the process of enumeration and their use it is necessary to have a thorough and clear reception of the 'Schedules'. For this purpose the classifier may see in the 'Schedule' the following :

1. the ten main classes.
2. the main division of each Main class
3. the main subdivisions of each main division.
4. the type of notation used.
5. the method of subdividing class.
6. The method and notation used for enumerating standard subdivision type classes.
7. the method and techniques used for sharpening, subdividing and individualising the classes, e.g. the Add Device, Alphabetical device etc.
8. the classes for which special auxiliary tables are provided.

4

Cataloguing

Introduction

The Library clientele is expected to use the collection of a library documents either for study or research or reference. At any one time, the user may not find all the documents on the shelf. In order to know the complete collection, reliance is placed on a dependable tool which is called the catalogue of the library. The library catalogue facilitates the use of library materials.

The 'Catalogue' may be regarded as a work in which contents are arranged in a reasonable way, according to a set plan or merely word by word. In fact the definition of catalogue is related to the very purpose of a catalogue. The catalogues are of various kinds—Library catalogues, booksellers catalogues, printers publishers catalogues etc. Here we are concerned with library catalogues.

The library catalogue is a "list of documents in a library or in a collection forming a portion of it. This concept of library catalogue thus involves three aspects viz. (i) list (ii) documents and (iii) holdings of a library or group of libraries.

The 'list' indicates some sort of arrangement according to a set plan. The "documents" refers to printed, handwritten and engraved materials, including books, periodical publications, microfilms, photographs, gramophone records, taperecords etc. The documents embrace all types and forms of records in which information can be stored.

A library catalogue contains documents, which form the holdings of a library. When a library catalogue lists holdings or part of holdings of two or more libraries, then it is known as a 'union catalogue'.

Importance of a Catalogue

A library catalogue is a must for a library, especially when the collection becomes large. A library without a catalogue is like a town which has been developed without a plan. In absence of catalogue, it would not be possible to know what is available and where. It is a key to the resource of a library and whatever might be the arrangement on shelves, a well made catalogue is able to identify (to a large extent) and retrieve the documents successfully.

The catalogue should be well made having comprehensive entries. The extent of the use of library resources depends greatly upon the quality of a library catalogue. A good catalogue enhances the reputation of a library. On the other hand, an incomplete or poor catalogue mars the reputation, misguides not only to users but also to reference librarians, book selection experts and order librarians.

Different Types of Catalogue

The 'Catalogue' is regarded as a "work in which contents are arranged in a reasonable way, according to a set plan or merely word by word." The catalogues are of various kinds—(1) Library catalogues, (2) book-sellers catalogues, (3) printers catalogues, (4) publisher's catalogues etc. Here we are concerned with library catalogues only. In simple terms, a library catalogue is a "list of documents in a library or is a collection forming a portion of it."

A library classification arranges books on the shelf in a helpful order, providing an approach through a subject usually. However, users are likely to seek documents in a collection through a variety of other approaches. It is only the library catalogues which can satisfy the other approaches by providing various kinds of entries.Whatever might be the arrangement on shelves, a well made catalogue is able to identify (to a large extent) and retrieve the documents successfully. The extent of the use of library resources depends greatly upon the quality of a library catalogue. A comprehensive catalogue enhances the reputation of a library.

The aims of the library catalogue are :

1. To enable a person to find a book of which
   (a) the author or
   (b) the title or
   (c) the subject is known.
2. To show what the library has
   (d) by a given author
   (e) on a given subject
   (f) in a given kind of literature.

The catalogues can be kept in the following forms :

(i) In a bound book form
(ii) In a computer
(iii) In the form of index card. The cards are held in metal or wooden trays which can hold large number of cards.

The interpolation of view cards is easy enough. The size of cards is usually 12.5 cm. x 20 cm. The trade name is cardex. The cardex can be arranged in the following forms :

(i) Author catalogue
(ii) Book name catalogue
(iii) Subjectwise catalogue — The alphabetical index to class numbers is of great help to the readers to find out the class number of any particular subject.

In addition there are also separate catalogues for deputation reports, M. Sc. and Ph. D. theses of scientists and foresters, books in languages other than English, machine readable data files, etc.

* Place Index to Conference, Proceedings is arranged alphabetically by names of places/venues where the conference was held. Under a particular place further arrangement is done chronologically.

* Key word Index to conference proceedings is arranged alphabetically by key words from the titles of the conferences, meetings etc. Under a particular key word further arrangement is done chronologically.

* Key word Index to special issues of Periodicals wherein cards having key words, from the topics of the special issues of journals such as "The Indian Foresters" are arranged alphabetically.

The card catalogue must be consulted to find out if the library has a particular book or not, or which are the books available in the Library on a subject or by a particular author, or the call (class) number which indicates the location of the book in the library.

Job of a Cataloguer

The person who prepares a catalogue is called a cataloguer. He studies the documents, records and interprets and follows the catalogue code to prepare a catalogue. The process of preparing a catalogue is termed cataloguing, which denotes the various processes involved in the preparation of entries and maintenance of a catalogue. The preparation and maintenance of a library catalogue requires understanding of documents and their authors. He should also know the needs of users. The scope of the work of a cataloguer can be enormous if the collection to be catalogued is a large one.

Sources of Information for a Cataloguer

There are variety of sources which a cataloguer can use to get the information he requires to prepare entries of a library catalogue. The work to be catalogued is considered the most important source of information. For this he should acquire book sense. He should be able to determine the essentials without waste of time and effort. A cataloguer must also be able to get the essence of a book by scanning the preface or introduction or summary chapter, or some other part of the text.

A document usually consists of the following parts :

(1) **Binding** : The binding may be of publisher's binding or binder's binding. The binding contains cover title, authors' name, publisher's symbol, publisher's name, and description of the author and the book.

(2) **Title page** : It is the most important source of information to a cataloguer. It is a page of document or a volume of its which usually contains full title, author's name, name of collaborators, publisher, place, date of publication etc.

(3) **Back of title page** : It usually contains information about edition, year of publication, year of copyright etc. It is considered a very useful source of information.

(4) **Dedication** : It is a kind of information by the author to someone else. It is placed on a page preceding the preface but is usually unimportant.

(5) **Preface** : The preface contains explanation by the author as to why he wrote the book. It also contains author's plan, explanation as to how the work was developed, and acknowledgement to those who might have assisted the author in the writing of the document. Preface can be highly useful because it can be helpful in knowing the scope, objectives and significance of the work. It precedes the table of contents.

(6) **Foreword or Introduction** : It is a preliminary note by some expert of the subject or eminent person in the praise of book and author. It follows the preface.

(7) **Table of contents** : It lists the contents of the document, often giving chapter headings, with or without explanations. It usually follows the foreword.

(8) **Text** : It contains the work proper and forms the most substantial portion of the document.

(9) **Index** : It is a detailed alphabetical list of names of persons, corporate bodies, places and subjects etc. dealt in the text, alongwith references to exact pages of occurrence.

(10) **Bibliography** : The bibliography is the list of books or documents used as references for writing the book. This may be included at the end of each chapter or at the end of the books or as footnotes.

The knowledge about the various parts of the document helps the cataloguer to obtain the information required for cataloguing, including relationship of the given document, with other documents and also in the identification of a document.

Descriptive Cataloguing

The various elements required for the descriptive cataloguing are :

(1) **Title** : This is the most important feature of a document. In computerised catalogue, it is the principal element for identification. An alternative title, if any, is included because the document might become better known in future through the alternative title rather than the original title.

(2) **Author's statement** : It is given after the title. The names of translator (s), editor (s), illustrator (s) etc. are also added after the title. There may be two or more authors.

(3) **Edition** : It is a must for a catalogue. However, information regarding impression or a reprint is ignored.

(4) **Imprint** : It includes place of publication, publisher's name, and date of publication and copyright. It helps in identification of different editions. Information about the publisher sometimes helps to confirm the degree of reliability of the work. Place of imprint can indicate biases and differences in terminology etc.

(5) **Collation** : It is concerned with pagination or number of volumes, illustrations, size etc. The number of volumes and indication about illustrations, if considered significant are regarded essential in an entry. For normal size, no symbol is to be used. In oversized books, book number is overlined and in undersized books, book number is underlined. Exact size is hardly of any significance in most cases except for publications like atlases etc.

(6) **Series** : The series is often referred by the users, especially casual readers. Sometimes it may give an indication about the level of the work. It helps in identification of an edition of a particular document. Series statement is very helpful to librarians for checking the catalogue to find out whether the library possesses a complete set in the series or not.

(7) **Notes** : The notes amplify or qualify formalized description, either when the rules do not permit the inclusion of the needed information in any form other than a note or when the incorporation or information in the formalized description would be misleading, cumbersome or inappropriate. The notes describe title, sub-title, alternative title, authorship, collaborators, edition, imprint, collation, series and additional physical description, bibliographical history, relationship to other works and to other editions of the same work contents (or partial contents), title romanized and literary form etc.

(8) **Annotation** : It may cover information about authorship, subject, relationship with other documents etc. Very few library catalogues include annotation. Certain notes—which provide necessary additional information relating to title, edition, imprint, collation, sometimes list of contents also fall within the scope of orthodox descriptive cataloguing. The annotation is an accurate and

compendious statement as to the subject scope, manner, qualifications of the author and general suitability of the book for this or that type of reader.

Order of Description in Cataloguing

The order of description of various elements usually consists of title, sub-title, alternative title, author statement, edition, imprint, collation, series, notes and annotation. The most important elements should be placed first because often the users read the first few lines of an entry.

Amount of information : The amount of information to be included in a catalogue entry depends on kind of library, availability of financial support, nature of the document, nature of catalogue etc. If the document is rare one, then more details would be required. In case it is decided to print the catalogue, consideration regarding space and cost would lead to provision of limited details. In a research library it might be essential to provide information about imprint, collation, and notes. The British standard, 1629 : 1950 Bibliographical references suggests author, title, date and series as the bare minimum.

Rules for filing entries

Once the entries are ready, these must be filed in an order into the catalogue. Filing means to arrange in an orderly manner. But this is not as simple as it might appear to be. The bigger the catalogue greater the problem. The greatest problem in alphabetization is whether to follow letter by letter or word by word or some other arrangement.There are a number of codes for filing such as American Library Association (ALA) rules for filing catalogue cards, British Standards Institution's Alphabetical arrangement, Indian Standards Institution's practice for alphabetical arrangement etc.

The entries in a classified art should be arranged by means of class numbers given in their leading sections.

Cataloguing of Non-Forestry Documents

In every forest library there will be forestry books as well as non-forestry books. For the forestry documents the classification and indexinng should be done as per "Oxford system of decimal classification." For non-forestry documents the alternative is either to follow universal Decimal Classificatio~ or to follow the classification based on accession number. The UDC is very comprehensive and difficult to follow therefore the best alternative is to arrange the documents accession numberwise.

(1) **English Section** : In this section all the English non-forestry books etc. will be kept and classified accession numberwise, for example (i) ES/1, (ii) ES/2, (iii) ES/3, and so on. (ES = English section.)

(2) **Hindi Section** : In this section all the Hindi language non-forestry books and other literatures would be kept and classified accession numberwise, for example (i) HS/1 (ii) HS/2, (iii) HS/3 and so on (HS = Hindi section).

(3) **Marathi Section** : In Marathi section all the Marathi language non-forestry documents would be kept and classified accession numberwise, e.g. (i) MS/1, (ii) MS/2, (iii) MS/3 and so on (MS = Marathi Section).

(4) **Bangla Section** : In Bangla section all the Bengali language non-forestry documents would be kept and classified according to accession number, e.g. (i) BS/1, (ii) BS/2, (iii) BS/3 and so on (BS = Bangla Section).

(5) **Tamil Section** : In Tamil Section all the Tamil language non-forestry documents would be kept and classified accession numberwise, e.g. (i) TS/1, (ii) TS/2, (iii) TS/3, (iv) TS/4 and so on.

Organisation of Cataloguing Work

There are two main patterns for organisation of work :—(1) All work of classifying, assigning subject headings, and descriptive cataloguing may be carried out by one person according to field of specialization, (2) The second pattern consists of one person being made responsible for classifying and assigning subjects headings and another person is responsible for descriptive cataloguing.

If the classification and cataloguing is done by different persons, then this will not be economical and will result in duplication of work. If classification and cataloguing is done by the same person, then work can be organised on a subject or language basis, with subject specialists in given fields working independently or in group. Under this arrangement, the cataloguers are likely to become narrow specialists. The distinction should be made between professional and non-professional jobs. The professionals should attend to professional work leaving non-professional work to be done by others. For instance, catalogues cards must be typed by a typist under the supervision of a professional. Checking of details from the catalogues could be done by a non-professional.

Guides Outside the Catalogue

By the side of the catalogue a notice should be provided containing basic instructions on the use of the catalogue.

The classified catalogue includes entries for all the books in the library. The catalogue is arranged in two parts : (a) The classified part, where the entries are arranged by call number. This arrangement is the same as that of documents on shelves (b) the alphabetical part containing entries under author (s), editor (s), translator (s), compiler (s), title, subject and services.

Explain the basis of arrangement giving suitable examples. Finally describe how the user should consult it, and get the maximum out of it. However the description should be brief, to the point and written in simple language easy to follow:

Maintenance of Catalogue

The maintenance of a library catalogue is very important. More and more books are added every year in the library and the filing becomes more difficult and time-consuming. The catalogue should be maintained in the following way :

(1) Replace soiled catalogues and guide cards on regular basis.

(2) A list of weak spots should be prepared and filing of cards should be reviewed on these points from time to time.

(3) The cards for books being released should be filed at the same time. If this is not possible then a supplementary file should be maintained and cards from these should be filed regularly.

(4) Subject headings and references should be kept up-to-date, replacing cards under out-of-date names of subjects and their references.

(5) Cards, which are no-longer useful should be removed. Similarly, cards for books withdrawn or lost should be removed from the catalogue.

Staff Manual

A staff manual is a must for a library especially for the technical section. It is a record of all the decisions, made during the course of day to day work. It may be maintained on cards or in a loose leaf note book. A manual should include processes and rules.

Authority File

The authority file is a record of the decisions taken by a cataloguer. Besides the staff manual, authority file used for recording decisions about individual items can be very useful. This helps in maintaining consistency in the rendering of headings—such as author heading, subject headings and references etc. There will be numerous decisions that are taken by cataloguers which do not find a place in the staff manual, which only provides the broad guidelines, leaving details to the authority file. For a classified catalogue, a file of cards may be prepared to indicate, which class index entries have already been made for each class number. The maintenance of authority file requires work experience.

Limited Cataloguing

Day by day increase in the amount of literature being published and its increasing complexity, the costs of cataloguing have been increasing steadily. Limited cataloguing is one approach to reduce costs, which refers "to any reductions in the amount of cataloguing." These reductions can take place in terms of number of entries and amount of information in each entry.

The limited cataloguing can take two forms viz. selective cataloguing and simplified cataloguing.

(a) **Selective cataloguing**: This is concerned with reduction in the number of entries for a document. In case subject and title entries are the same, title entry can be avoided. Even otherwise, title entry is often prepared in case of those documents where a user is likely to remember the title. Joint author, Joint editor, Joint translator, and Joint illustrator entries are often omitted. If a book deals with three or more sub-divisions of a subject, then an entry is prepared under the general heading and references are made to satisfy other approaches.

(b) **Simplified cataloguing :** This is concerned with reduction in the descriptive cataloguing as well as simplification of heading. It is essential that a cataloguer must limit the provision of description to items which are essential for the identification of particular editions of a given document being catalogued. In this connection a cataloguer should always ask himself whether all the details that he is including are really necessary. The catalogue is expected to provide so much information as is necessary for the purpose of identifying the document e.g. Author, title and even notes (in a few cases) are considered sufficient to constitute the data bank for identification purposes. Whereas a detailed catalogue contains maximum information about the document including the publisher, place of publication, size, pages, notes etc.

The limited cataloguing provides great scope for economy in cataloguing thus reducing the cost but increasing the output of cataloguing. However, it should not be practised at the cost of service to users or for the sake of short-term gains. It is accepted that in a close-access library more information in entries is necessary than in an open-access library, because in a close access library the catalogue will be the only source which will help users in the retrieval of documents.

Symbiosis Between a Catalogue and Classification

Classification arranges documents on the shelf or entries in a classified catalogue according to a filiatory sequence. On the other hand, cataloguing involves preparation of a library catalogue which serves as a key to the resources of the library. Both classification and cataloguing aim to get every reader his or her document and every document to its reader. For a long time both were developed independently. Later it was realized that a catalogue is directly complementary to classification and the two should be developed on the basis of mutual relationship to the benefit of both. This kind of mutually beneficial partnership between classification and a catalogue is termed symbiosis which is essential for the healthy growth of efficient library services. The classifier and cataloguer help each others:

(a) **Help provided by a classifier to a cataloguer :** The entries in the classified part of the classified catalogue are arranged by means of a class number or a call number provided by a classifier.

The leading section of the main entry in a classified catalogue is a 'call number' or 'class number'. The efficiency of the cataloguing is dependent on the scheme of classification. While using a list of subject headings, the specific subject of the document is determined by a classifier at the time, he classifies the document. This saves the time of the cataloguer.

(b) **Help provided by a cataloguer to a classifier :** A classification scheme arranges documents on the shelf so as to be most useful to the readers. The arrangement of documents on shelves reveals only those documents which are lying on the shelves at that time. Therefore, it is only the library catalogue which can reveal the entire resources of the library including the documents that have been loaned out, or misplaced by the readers. There are many documents which cover more than one subject. It would not be possible to purchase as many copies of a document, as there are subjects it deals with and allot it to different subjects. The only feasible solution is to enter the document in the catalogue under as many subject heading(s) as necessary. Composite books often require such a treatment. A reader may approach by remembering author, editor, translator, title, or series etc. In such cases, classification is of no help. But library catalogue can provide the answer. The classification arranges documents according to thought content, whereby works by the same author or belonging to the same series get scattered. It is only the catalogue which brings such documents together.

5

Classified Catalogue Code

According to Dr. Ranganathan "A catalogue code is like a legal document. Any rule in it should be interpreted like a legal text." A classified catalogue comprises of two parts, viz. classified and Alphabetical.

Entries : The library catalogue comprises of various unit records prepared for each of the documents under call number. author, title and various other headings to satisfy the different approaches of the users.

Varieties of entry are mainly two :

(i) Main Entry and

(ii) Added entry.

Main entry : It contains all necessary information required for complete individualization of a document. The extent of information to be provided in Main Entry would depend upon the cataloguing policy of the library and the nature of the document catalogued. The main entry is also known as comprehensive entry or the fullest entry for a document. It is the basic entry which contains data for most of the added entries. All the other entries - specific or general relating to the document are normally derived from the main entry.

Added entries : According to CCC - the entry other than main entry is an Added Entry. These are secondary entries which are provided under various headings and the Class Number of a guest document. These entries assist to know whether the desired document is available in the library and, if available what is its relative location alongwith other documents on the library shelves.

Structure of the Catalogue Card :

In modern libraries, catalogue card is the most popular. A single entry is provided on each of the card, which can be arranged in any desired manner. The blank, fully ruled and partially ruled cards are in use in different libraries. In case of ruled cards, there are two vertical guidelines and one horizontal guideline. The first vertical line is known as 'First indention' and the second vertical line is known as 'Second indention'. These can be adjusted on typewriting machine by making 8 and 13 spaces if blank catalogue cards are used. The horizontal guideline is known as the 'Leading Section'. All these lines are provided in red while the other horizontal lines are provided in light black or light blue.

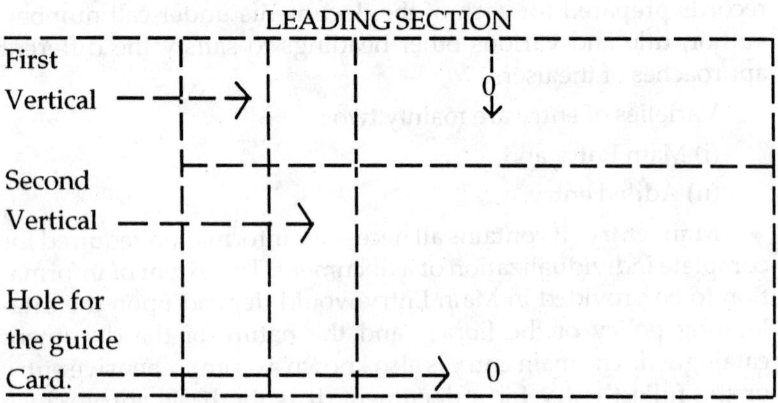

Fig. 1 : A Catalogue Card

The general norms to be remembered in respect of the guidelines are :

(i) As the entries are arranged under the information occupying the Leading Section, the most important information should be provided in the Leading Section. The information occupying the Leading Section always starts from the First Vertical.

(ii) All new sections, except the Accession Number section in Main Entry, Index Number Section and the series Number in the second section of the Book Index Entry should start from the second vertical.

(iii) If it is not possible to accommodate all the information in a section in one horizontal line, it may be continued in the next lower line starting from the First Vertical.

General Norms of Recording

The classified catalogue code (C C C) prescribes the following norms :

(a) **Call Number/Index Number**

The call number is specific for each document. It consists of Class Number and Book Number. In the Main Entry it occupies the Leading Section. When call number appears in any section other than the Leading section in Added Entries it is known as Index Number.

(b) **Heading**

Heading is the most important part of the entry. It consists of word groups representing the name of person(s), Place(s), Corporate body (ies), Title, series and subjects etc. under which various entries can be provided.

The heading occupies second section in the Main Entry of the classified catalogue whereas call Number occupies the Leading Section or the First Section.

(c) **Other Sections**

The Accession Number should be provided, if ruled cards are used on the bottom-most line of the card between two verticals. In case of blank cards its place may be appropriately adjusted. Accession number is lengthy, it may be allowed to flow out of the second vertical line. In case of multi-volumed and multiple copies Accession Numbers should be provided in the sequence parallel to the sequence of the Book Numbers e.g.

....

....

....

841, 1232 - 3

Here, 841 is the Accession Number of the first copy and 1232, 1233 are that of second and third copy respectively. The numbers' continuation should be mentioned connected with a dash but without repeating, the common numbers. The numbers not in continuation should be separated by a comma.

(d) **Directing element**

In added entries, necessary Directing Elements are used. The purpose of the directing word or phrase is to direct the users of the catalogue to the appropriate heading or the class number to find out the specific information in the catalogue, 'see' and 'see also' are used as Directing elements to refer from the alphabetical, headings to another such headings.

Structure of the main entry

The structure of the main entry is as under :

		Call number
		Heading
		Title, Ed, Collaborators
		(Series)
		Other notes, if any.
		Accession Number

General Guidelines for Cataloguing

The Call Number consists of Class Number and Book Number. Each book bears a call number label on its spine. The year of publication should be given in the case of books and the year in the case of conference proceedings, denoting as the book number. The letter A is used to represent the digits '19' in the years 1901 to 1999.

Examples :

(1) First edition of a simple one volume book - the book number to be derived from the year of publication :

(i) Techniques in Seed Science and Technology 1987 :

Call Number → 232.3 ← Class Number
A 87 ← Book Number

(ii) Soil microorganisms and Plant growth - 1977.

114.6
A - 77

(2) More than one book having the same class number and published in the same year. All the following books have the same call number 61 and are published in the same year 1986.

1st Book added to the library-Book no, A 86

2nd book -- A 861

10th Book -- A 869

11th book -- A 869.1

12th book -- A 869.2

(3) Various editions of the same book :

Plant diseases by R.S. Singh.

1st ed. (1968)	2nd ed. (1969)	3rd ed. (1971)
444	444	444
A 68	A 68:A 69	A 68:A 71

(4) Conference proceedings - unnumbered conference.

Proceedings of the Third Silvicultural Conference.

—Dehradun - 1929.

2 : (042)
A 29

The book number for a conference is to be derived from the year of conference. The years of actual publication is ignored.

(5) Numbered conferences having the same name and the same subjects :-

Call number	Title
2 : (042) A 18: A 51	Proceedings of the Silvicultural Conference -8th-Dehradun-1951.
2 : (042) A 18 : A 56	Proceedings of the Silvicultural Conference - 9th-Dehradun-1951.
2 : (042) A18 : A 67	Proceedings of the Silvicultural Conference - 11th-Dehradun-1951.

The basic book number is constructed from the year of the first conference. The first conference was held in 1918. Therefore, the basic book number is A18.

(6) For more detailed cataloguing the class number, Author mark and Accession number are written on the catalogue as below :

Plant Protection in India by D.B. Reddy, 1968.

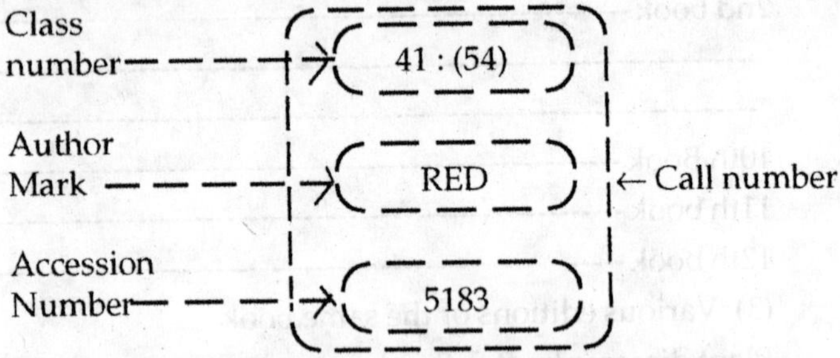

(7) The author mark and book number can be clubbed together so that card-catalogue may become more explicit.

Advances in Forest Genetics by P.K. Khosla - 1981
(Ambika Publications, New Delhi)

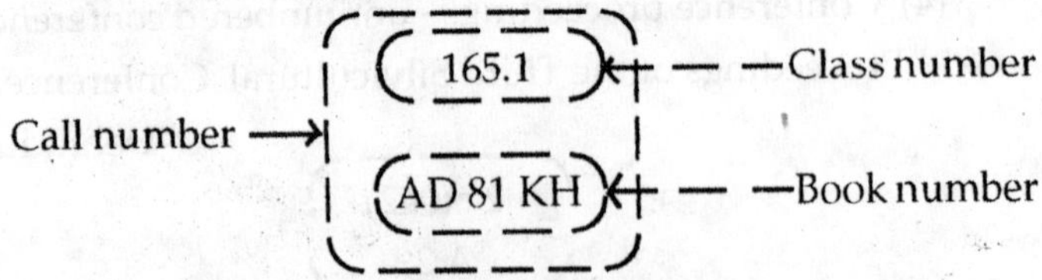

The same book if arranged according to the name of author in card catalogue will have call number as under :

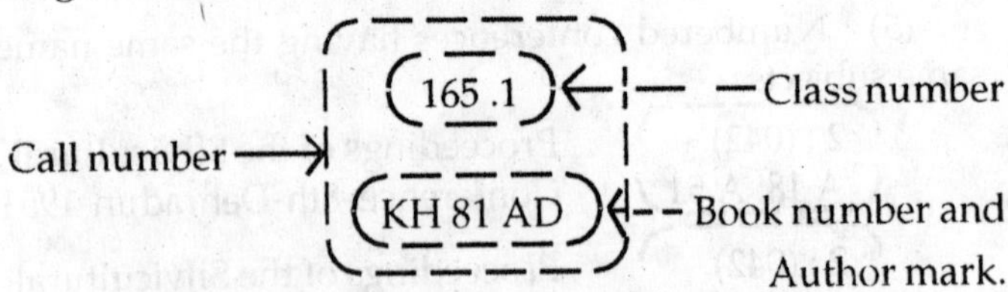

(B) Some books have two or more authors, in such cases the name of first author may be sufficient for book number or all the authors may also be used for book number.

Methods of soil Analysis - 1973 by Black C.A. and Evans D.D.

The call number will be

114.21	← Class number
ME 73 BLA	← Book number and author mark
ME 73 BLA EVA	← Call number

The whole card then will be written as,

114.21	Methods of soil analysis - 1973 Cost Rs. 526/-
Me 73	BLACK C.A. & EVANS D.D.
BLACK EVA	(American Society of Agronomy Wisconstin-
	USA)

Types of Documents

The various types of documents that are kept in the Library are :

(1) **Books** : The books are arranged on the shelves in the order of their UDC/ODC and book numbers. Labels are pasted on the racks to facilitate location of the books. The principal sources for locating the books is the card catalogue which can also be made available on-line on any of the computer terminals located in the library.

(2) **Reference Collection** : A number of important books and costly documents are set aside for reference purposes only. These are also arranged according to the UDC/ODC system. These documents are always available for reference purposes. It should be ensured that duplicate copies are available in the regular collection meant for circulation.

(3) **Recent Arrival Display Unit** : New books added to the library should be displayed every Monday for a week. New books can be reserved from issuing provided they are not reference books. If there are more than ten reservations for a new book, then it is

released for circulation only after a month during which the period will be available for reference in the library. Unreserved books should be issued after the display period is over.

(4) **Conference Proceedings** : Proceedings of conferences are also classified and arranged alongwith other books using ODC systems. The conference proceedings are normally published as a book, or as a part of a periodical in its regular issues or as a special supplement.

Some of the guides to conference proceedings like *Inter Dok Directory of Published Proceedings* (Inter D.K. Corporation New York) and *Index of Conference Proceedings Received* (The British Library Document' supply centre, Boston spa, UK) assist the reader to know whether the proceedings of a particular conference have been published or whether meetings have been held in the past in a particular subject field.

(5) **Technical Reports** : The technical reports have the advantage of rapid publication and dissemination as compared to journal articles and books.

(6) **Tapes** : Video tape collection and audio cassettes should be maintained and used in the library premises only.

(7) **Periodicals** : The foreign and Indian journals should be displayed in the library in four different groups.

(a) Current Issues of Periodicals

Wrich's International Periodicals Directory : Which is a classified guide to current periodicals : Foreign and Domestic (3- vols, Bowker, New York) will help a reader to find periodicals covering a given subject and to find details of publisher, frequency and cost and also to find out which A & I journals cover a particular periodical. The bibliographical data of Indian journals can also be obtained from *Directory of Indian Scientific Periodicals* (INSDOC, New Delhi). *National Union Catalogue of Scientific Serials in India.* (INSDOC, New Delhi) gives the list of journal holdings of various libraries throughout the country.

(b) **Bound Volumes of Back issues of periodicals** : When all the issues comprising one complete volume of a Journal are received in the library, they are bound along with the index to the volume and shifted to the area where bound volumes of back issues are shelved. The arrangement of back volumes are also alphabetical, according to the title of the journal, and is chronological within the set.

(c) **Abstracting and Indexing Journals :** These journals are displayed separately in alphabetical order by title. Their back issues are also bound and shelved.

Abstracting journals provide information under various subject headings, abstracts of journal articles, reports etc. together with the relevant bibliographic information for each item. Most of the A & I journals have at least an author and subject indices. A & I journals are useful for retrospective searches of published literature in a given subject field. They are also useful in keeping in touch with the work of an individual scientist. In addition to printed versions which may become less and less popular the information on CD-ROMs should also be made available.

(d) **Current contents :** There is a considerable time lag, sometimes 2 years, or even more before an article published in a primary source gets included in an A & I journal. Therefore certain CAS (Current Abstracting Services) should be developed. An example of this is 'current contents' of Institute for Scientific Information, Philadelphia, USA published weekly in different subject fields. Each issue contains the content pages of the most recent issues of selected Journals.

(e) **Other Materials** : The other publications like standards, patents, deputation reports, theses, books in languages other than English and trade literature are also maintained in the library. Separate catalogues should be maintained for these. Newspaper clippings on selected topics should also be filed separately.

6

Filing Systems

Introduction

All the auxiliaries are applied for the formation of compound UDC or ODC numbers for subjects which have not been enumerated in UDC or ODC tables. The filing or listing order of such compound UDC or ODC numbers needs to be explained for indicating how documents have to be arranged on shelves; cabinets or folders. The alignment of UDC numbers follows from general (less restrictive) to particular (more restrictive). The filing order of documents bearing both simple and compound numbers follows a set of principles which can be enunciated as follows:

Coordination / addition symbol +, consecutive extension symbol /, relation symbol : and order fixing symbol : : which interlinks or interrelates simple UDC number to form compound UDC numbers.

The Common Auxiliaries, which are least restrictive, are filed before others with more general meanings. Thus, these independent auxiliaries, which can be used alone or cited first, are followed by non-consecutive aggregation or consecutive extension of several numbers. These, in turn, have a concept which is broader than that of a simple number. This means that compound numbers with the plus, the stroke and the colon are filed before a single component with more restrictive meaning. For example, 53 + 54 will be filed before 53.

A number with an auxiliary as suffix has more restrictive

meaning than a simple number and will, therefore, be filed after the simple number. For example 524 will be filed before 524.4, or 111.1 will be filed before 114.41.

As the division of main clâsses follows a hierarchical pattern, a succession of digits interposed with decimal points make the meaning of UDC or ODC number more and more restrictive. In other words the base remaining the same, the longer the number the more restrictive is the concept. In such a situation, shorter numbers will logically be filed before longer ones e.g.

232	Artificial regeneration.
232.1	Choice and trial of species, races etc. (Provenance trials etc.)
232.2	Preparatory works, auxiliary measures, (site preparation etc.)
232.3	Seed, Nursery practice, direct sowing.
232.31	Seed (Plus trees, elite trees, seed orchards, seed collection, storage etc.)
232.321	Nursery sites, including factors affecting selection of sites for nurseries.
232.328	Vegetative propagation.
232.329	Miscellaneous. (Green houses, heated frames, cold frames etc.)

ODC class numbers are mostly numerical consisting of Arabic numerals. The arrangement (or filing order) of UDC numbers thus become mechanical more so because decimal functions possess an inherent ordinal value e.g.

811	Structure, identification.
811.1	Anatomical elements and tissues.
811.2	Special features and abnormal structure (anatomical aspects)
811.4	Growth rings.
811.5	Sapwood and heartwood.
811.6	Texture, grain, figure
811.7	Phloem, bark.
811.9	Miscellaneous.

Non-numerical and other symbols are given an arbitrary ordinary value which are filed immediately after the symbol e.g. " " (double quotation marks).

Meanwhile, the implications that arise in terms of filing the entries (or documents) when more than one auxiliary are used need to be explained. For example :

160 "17" Plant Chemistry — 18th century AD

160 (54) Plant Chemistry — India.

The citation of special and common auxiliary subdivisions and symbols follows a reverse order in a UDC number for a compound or complex subject, for example the common auxiliary for time will be preceded by the that place, e.g.

160 (54) "17" Plant Chemistry — India — 18th century AD

The filing order of these three UDC numbers will be as follows :—

160 "17" Plant chemistry — 18th century AD

160 (54) Plant chemistry — India.

160 (54) "17" Plant chemistry — India— 18th century AD

This example indicates that by subordinating the time to place, a general before—special sequence has been maintained.

A compound UDC number can be formed using colon as a facet indicator even when special auxiliaries exist for introducing the same concept. A few examples will clarify the point when special auxiliaries are used to formulate number:

232.31 - - 01 Research and Testing of seed. - - 01 auxiliary is used for Research and Testing)

When colon is used, the number denoting the same concept becomes.

232.31 : 23 - - 01 Seed - Research and Testing.

Table 1 : Filing of Auxiliaries

Filing or listing of compound UDC numbers less restrictive to more restrictive.

Common Auxiliary Signs

Auxiliary Signs	*Significance*
+(Plus)	for coordination, addition
/ (stroke)	for consecutive extension

0 — 9	Simple main number
: (colon)	for relation
[ ] (square brackets)	for subgrouping
: : (double colon)	for order-fixing

Independent Auxiliary Signs

=	Language
(01/09)	Form
(1/9)	Place
(=...)	race (Not of much relevance in forestry)
" .... "	time (—do—)
A/Z	non UDC numbers (—do—)

Dependent Auxiliary Signs

.00	Point of view, materials and person. (Not of much relevance in forestry)

Special Auxiliary Signs

-1/-9	hyphen series	(denote recurring concepts and not of much relevance in forestry)
.01/.09	point-nought series	
'1/'9	apostrophe series	

Note :— (1) The common auxiliaries 'place' may follow 'time' in filing order if the former is considered to be more restrictive than the latter.

(2) *_______ is used for adding non UDC notations, for example * 3 _______ the third and *245 Tending of trees.

The sign = signifies parallel division, and indicates that the subdivisions of the number following the sign can be used to formulate new numbers which are not present in the schedule. This is done by taking some digits from the end of this number (Known as the source number) and adding them to the number preceding the sign =. This number is known as the target number. The significance of the parallel division will be apparent from the following example :

232.04 = 263.04

The source number 232.04 denotes protection of Artificial Regeneration while the target number 263.04 indicates protection of irrigated forests.

Use of Suare Brackets : The number which is kept within spuare brackets connotes three different meanings;

(a) Number not to be used : If number is within square brackets it means the number is no longer in vogue and therefore should not be used for classifying the documents on the subject which is mentioned against this bracketed number. Therefore, in place of this bracketed number the alternate class number provided under this number should be used. For example.

(1) 18 th Ed	19 th Ed
114	[114]

(b) For Subgrouping : When a compound number denoted by two or more numbers, are linked together by plus or colon, and the resultant number, in turn, is related to another number by colon (or modified by common or special auxiliary), the square bracket symbol is used for subgrouping the concepts, e.g.

(100.2) (213) : [83 : 972 ITTO] International Tropical Timber Organisation.

(084.122) : [(213) : 61 film] A film about Tropical Forest Management.

(c) For Irreversible Computerised Information : When the component numbers in a compound is fixed by double colon symbol : : (for order fixing) the arrangement becomes irreversible. The double colon and square bracket is useful in an UDC classified collection of computerised information retrieval system. In such case, the aforesaid subject will be denoted by the following number.

(100.2) (213) : : [83 : 972 ITTO] International Tropical Timber Organisation.

(084.122) : : [213 : 61 film] A film about Tropical Forest Management.

Summary : Summing up the preceding matter, it can be stated that the UDC-ODC inherits the ingenious features of the DDC in allowing its classes to be divided and subdivided to any extent. Though somewhat restricted in scope due to its narrow base, the UDC is capable of designating all compound and complex subjects through the application of connecting symbols, common and special auxiliaries, and a number of innovative devices. In UDC, characteristics that are common to many categories are identified which are then arranged into lists (or tables), each of these representing a facet subjects thus get analysed into their constituent elements which can later be combined and reconstituted in the form of class numbers to designate them. The UDC can be conveniently adapted to computerised files.

7

Retrieval Languages

Introduction

The major utility of a classification scheme rests on the feasibility of its use for ISR (Information Storage and Retrieval system). The indexing and retrieval languages, which appear to be peripheral, is as important as the classification itself. The documents arranged according to the class numbers can be retrieved easily. But class numbers which consists of digits, convey their significance only to those who are familiar with the Classification Schedule. These numbers have to be interpreted in terms of words which are comprehensible to all. The traditional form of retrieval in libraries is done with the help of catalogues which have several forms and formats. One of these is the classified catalogue which consists of three parts, i.e. classified file, Author/Title index (A/Z) and A/Z subject index.

In the author/title index (A/Z), the entries are prepared according to the names of authors and the titles of documents are filed in an alphabetical order. The users should know at least one of these indications to locate the document. The index is generally kept separate from the A/Z subject index.

This retrieval system can be represented through the following diagram :

Classified Catalogue

- Classified file
  - Single Entry System.
  - Double Entry System.
- Author/Title index (A/Z)
- A/Z Subject index.

The A/Z subject index serves as a guide to the classified file because it is the key to the location of a topic and is a reference to the names of subjects from their numbers.

Library Extension Service

The objectives of an extension service is to convert a library into a social, cultural and intellectual centre which encourages reading. Thus an extension service aims at converting non-readers into readers. This is done by bringing books and readers together.

The various extension services that a forest library can offer are:

(i) **Organising reading circles** : Persons with common subject interest may be brought together by the library to a reading circle. Each reading circle should be given necessary facilities regarding reading materials and a suitable place to hold the meetings.

The forest libraries should hold at least two reading circles every year for at least 30 persons at a time.

(ii) **Arranging meeting place for NGOs or local Learned Organizations :—**

The libraries at the divisional level as well as at the Conservator level should arrange meetings of NGOs etc. to encourage better social and personal contacts. This should be done once in a year.

(iii) **Lectures and Talks :** The library should organise lectures and talks by eminent foresters, scientists and superior officers. The subjects to be chosen should be of wide range with special reference to current topics. On each occasion the information about books available in the library on the concerned topics should be announced.

(iv) **Cultural Programme** : The library may arrange music concert or film show on forestry topics.

(v) **Exhibitions** : At the time of the lecture, talk or film show etc., a book exhibition on the forestry topic may be organised. If necessary the books can be issued on the spot or may be reserved for issue latter. While organising book exhibitions, not only the books but other kinds of documents such as charts, posters, magazines, manuscripts, graphs, microfilms, photographs, etc. can also be displayed. The display must be related to the kind of activity being organised and level and needs of the group of readers concerned. The display must be attractive.

8

Library Staff and Administration

Introduction

Staffing function is an extremely important function. It aims to obtain competent personnel and provides favourable environment most conductive for superior performance. 'Vidya-dan' i.e. imparting of knowledge has been considered as the most sacred task in Ancient India and Manu rightly allotted this job to the most gifted persons of the society of that age. Gurudeva Tagore rightly had remarked, "The extent of use to which the reading material of a library is put, should determine its importance rather than the staggering number of volumes." He deprecated the idea of putting more emphasis on collecting books alone. In ultimate analysis, the future of any organisation depends more on quality of the personnel rather than any other single element.

According to Luther Gulick the library administration stands for the following functions :

1. Planning
2. Organising
3. Staffing
4. Directing
5. Co-ordinating
6. Reporting
7. Budgeting.

Categories of Staff

The staff in a library may be divided into the following three categories :

(a) Professional (b) Supporting (technical)/para-professional and (c) Supporting (administrative).

(a) Professional : Professional staff consists of those who are employed on professional jobs and possess degrees in library science as well as in some other discipline. These are further classified into professional senior, professional junior and professional assistant.

In absence of any trained person, the Assistant Conservator of Forests and Range Forest Officers as they are science graduates and trained in the science of forestry can do this job very well. The following is the list of jobs which can be performed by Assistant Conservator of Forests and Range Forest Officers :

Book selection, Book order, Classification, Cataloguing, Indexing, Abstracting, Reference service/information service and planning.

(b) Supporting staff (technical) : Supporting staff (technical) can be compared to para-medical staff employed in a hospital, e.g. nurses, X-ray technicians etc. These play an important role in the working of a library. They should possess a library qualification, of the level of certificate in Library science. In addition, one should be a matriculate. Our foresters and accountants are technically competent to do this job which involves following works :

(1) Preparation of book selection slips after the items have been marked, (2) Accessioning of books, (3) Registration of periodical volumes, (4) numbering work (jacket, inside, tag and date label numbering), (5) charging and discharging of books, (6) maintenance of issue-records, (7) documentation lists etc., (8) shelving of books and periodicals, (9) preparation of books and periodicals for binding and stock-taking.

(c) Supporting (administrative) : The nature of jobs carried out by supporting staff (administrative) is such that these are usually done in the office of any institution. There is nothing special about them. One clerk-cum-typist can do this job. The following is the list of jobs, which are usually performed by the supporting staff (administrative) :

(1) Secretarial assistance to the librarian, (2) maintenance of accounts and stores, (3) salaries of staff, (4) purchase of stores, (5) maintenance of stock registers for both consumable and non-consumable articles, (6) payment of bills etc., (7) typing of catalogue cards, bibliographies, documentation lists, and (8) day to day correspondences.

In view of the supra, the following staff can be appointed or engaged for the forest library :

(I) Conservator of Forests Office Library.

Library Authority—Conservator of Forests.

(a)	Librarian	-	Assistant Conservator of Forests	— One
(b)	Assistant Librarian	-	Range Forest Officer	— One
(c)	Junior Librarian	-	Accountant/Forester	— One
(d)	Library Assistant	-	Clerk cum typist	— One
(e)	Peon	-	One.	
	Total	-	5 (Five) Persons.	

(II) Dy. Conservator of Forests Office Library.

Library Authority — Dy. Conservator of Forests.

(a)	Librarian	-	Range Forest Officer	— One
(b)	Assistant Librarian	-	Forester	— One
(c)	Junior Librarian	-	Clerk cum typist	— One
(d)	Peon	-	One.	
	Total	-	4 (Four) Persons.	

Proposed Library Committees in the Forest Department

A Library committee should be formed in the Forest Department for each library for the smooth functioning of the Library.

The library committees should meet two times in a year. The matters to be considered at the meetings should be clearly listed in succinct words and the relevant files should be kept at the hands of a Librarian. The committees shall finalise the matters pertaining to list of books for approval, purchase of stationery and other equipments, Bills, estimates of heavy plants or alterations in the building, readers services, staff etc.

Power and Functions of the Library Committees

The powers and functions of all the three library committees mentioned above would relate to the following items:

1. **Library Building** : The committee should ensure that a library building is functional and modular if proper library services are to be provided to the readers. It must provide natural light and fresh air.

2. **Library furniture and fittings** : The committee will ensure that adaquate, proper and cosy library fittings and furniture articles are made available in the library. Only standard furniture articles should be provided so that in future any number of identical articles may be added without any dislocation or wastage of money or space.

3. **Library staff** : Only interested and competent staff should be appointed.

4. **Library finance and Book collection** : The committee should provide enough funds for purchasing the basic book collection and for adding latest books in a library. The library committee can appoint a 'sub-committee' to serve as Book Selection Committee so that list of books are thoroughly scrutinized to avoid the purchase of undesirable books.

5. **Library Rules** : The library committee should frame a set of rules which are not rigid but are flexible and best suit the needs of the readers. Efforts should be made to have as few and simple rules as possible.

6. **Library Services** : The committee should put in its best efforts to secure full coverage and standard library service by providing better and more books and other facilities.

7. **Library policies** : The committee should lay down a policy for the guidance of the librarian for the general day-to-day administration in the library.

Functional Arrangement

The functional arrangement should be followed in the forest department libraries which would facilitate smooth functioning of the library. The functional arrangement includes following sections in the library :

(i) Documentation centre.

(ii) Reference Section — Reference, circulation and periodicals sections.

(iii) Technical section — Acquisition, cataloguing (Classification and cataloguing) and maintenance section.

(iv) Administrative section — Buildings, Stationery, Accounts and Personnel sections.

9

Library Financing Budgeting and Accounting

Introduction

Finance is the motive power. It is essential for running any machinery properly. The following are the concepts underlying while making provision for library finance :

1. **Spending Institutions :** Libraries are not the revenue fetching agencies. Rather they are spending institutions because these take the nature of nation-building departments. It can be said that the libraries are the very basic of sound natural building activities.

2. **Growing institutions :** It implies that books, readers, staff, building and furniture requirements will go on increasing day by day since hundreds of books on forestry are being published every year which are to be ultimately acquired in libraries. To organise these books and other kindred materials for use, more staff, building and furniture will be required which can be procured if increased financial grant is given regularly.

3. **Financial demands are recurring :** Libraries are not only growing institutions but these once established will stay there for ever. Since books etc. are to be purchased every year adequate funds must be tapped for this purpose.

4. **Full coverage and standard library service :** For the development of mental faculties it is necessary to see that forest staff is provided with adequate and standard library service. Therefore sufficient expenses on recurring basis is needed.

Sources of Finance

The following can be the possible sources of finance or revenue :

(i) Subscription from members.
(ii) Government grants.
(iii) Library fines and fees.
(iv) Endowment and private donations.
(v) Gifts (Cash or kind)
(vi) Sale of publications (if any).
(vii) Income from reprographic services, translation services, compilation of bibliographies etc.

Methods of Financial Estimation

The following are the three methods of finding out the amount of finance required for providing satisfactory library service :

(i) **Per capita method :** In this method, a minimum amount per head of population is fixed which is considered essential for providing standard library service. The minimum is fixed taking into account the figures arrived at by means of cost accounting. The salary levels of the library staff in relation to other services and the average cost of publications are taken into account for determining this per capita limit.

Example : Let us suppose that in a divisional library it is considered that expenditure on documents per staff is Rs. 100. The total number of staff in the division being 420, then expenditure on reading material will be 100 x 420 = 42,000 (35% of total)

Staff Salary	Rs.	60,000	(50% of total)
Expenditure on equipments	Rs.	10,800	(9% of total)
Other Miscellaneous Expenditure	Rs.	7,200	(6% of total)
	Total Rs.	1,20,000	

(ii) **Proportional (method)** : In proportional method, the norm is laid down on the basis of total budget or research expenditure. According to Kothari Commission "6.5 per cent of educational budget is reasonable expenditure on libraries. But this could vary, say from 6.5 per cent to 10 per cent depending upon the stage of development of each university library. At the early stage of development, percentage may go upto 10 per cent."

(iii) **Methods of detail** : In this method all items of expenditure are accounted for while preparing financial estimates for a library. These items besides others include salaries / wages reading materials — books, periodicals, and newspapers and other kindred materials, binding and repairing, heating, cooling and lighting. Rents and interests; posts, telegraphs and telephones; and stationery and other contingent and miscellaneous items.

The Dy. C.Fs and CFs may formulate their report regarding the requirement of finance for each financial year.

Budgeting

A budget is an estimate of revenue and expenditure for the coming year. Estimates of possible income and expenditure of future year / years are reckoned and proper means for providing the requisite amounts are tapped. As budget is an estimate therefore it can be altered if the circumstances change. It needs to be flexible enough to meet the changing needs. On the other hand an annual finance report or statement tells us as to what was achieved as well as what could not be done last year.

(A) Factors Affecting Budget

The budget is affected by the following factors —

(i) Size of library in terms of collection, users, staff and scale of its operation,

(ii) Location and its physical arrangement,

(iii) Kinds of Library services,

(iv) Types of users served,

(v) Rising costs, and

(vi) Period covered (usually it will be one year).

(B) Budgeting Techniques

(i) **Line - item** : This is the most common type of budget. Here the expenditure is divided into broad categories such as—

(a) Salary and Wages,

(b) Books, periodicals and other reading materials,

(c) Equipment,

(d) Heating, Binding, Lighting, Water and Telephone,

(e) Stationery, Printing, Supplies, Insurance, and

(f) Miscellaneous.

It is possible to list items within broad categories. The line item budget is easy to prepare, justify and understand. Reallocation of funds can be done provided authorities agree to this.

(ii) **Lump sum** : In this method, a certain amount of money is allocated to the library. The library decides as to how that amount is going to be allocated to different categories. This gives considerable freedom to a librarian to allocate funds.

(iii) **Formula budgets** : Here a predetermined standards or formulas are applied for allocation of money. The formula is mechanical and easy to prepare.

(iv) **Performance budgeting** : It "bases expenditures on the performance of activities and emphasizes efficiency of operations." It gives justification for the description of services to be achieved by the proposed programme. Here the data is required for describing in detail.

The resources — (Men, materials and money) are required to accomplish the proposal and extent of programme to be achieved during the next fiscal year. Complicated techniques of cost benefit analysis are employed to measure performance and established norms.

(v) **Programme budgeting** : Here we are concerned with activities of the organisation but individual items or expenditures are ignored. The amounts are allocated to programmes or services rendered. It does not require expensive cost measurement studies implied in the performance bedget.

(C) General Standard of Budgeting

In view of the recommendations of various library experts and university and education commissions, the allocation of expenditure amongst various heads may be done on the following lines :

1. Salaries and Wages 50%
2. Books 20%
3. Periodicals 13%
4. Binding 7%

5. Lighting, Heating and Cooling etc. 3%
6. Library supplies and other Miscellaneous charges. 7%

The recurring and non-recurring expenditures may be segregated as under :

(a) Recurring

1. Salaries and Wages
2. Books
3. Periodicals
4. Binding
5. Lighting, Heating and Cooling etc.
6. Library supplies and other Miscellaneous charges.

(b) Non-Recurring

1. Initial book stock.
2. Furniture, fittings and equipments.
3. Library building.

10

Selection or Purchase of Books

Factors for Selection

The selection automatically implies rejection. Selection and rejection are only two ways of looking at the same operation. The selection or purchase of book involves judgement for which the following points should be considered.

(i) **Personal Inspection :** A book can be evaluated by actual examination for which the book must be seen and perused. The title alone may be a misleading criteria. The books can be inspected in a shop or in a book fair. However, India being a big country inspection of all the books before purchase is not possible.

(ii) **Budget :** The books should not be purchased hurriedly in the fag end of a financial year simply because the funds are available. This is nothing but self-deception. Since our main book markets are at Dehradun and Delhi which are more than thousands kms. away for many states, the account and audit rules should be amended in respect of surrender of unspent balance if this self-deception is to be avoided.

In order to utilize the library funds in a meaningful manner the unspent balance of the budget allotment for books in one year should be added to the budget allotment for books in the succeeding year.

(iii) **Dependence on review :** In absence of facility for the book selector to peruse the worth-while books, the next best is to depend on evaluation or review of the books appearing in periodicals etc. or as narrated by the competent or expert persons.

(iv) **Reputation of Author or Publisher :** The reputation of the author or publisher can be a good guide for the purchase of books.

(v) **Selection by the Committee :** The costly books costing more than Rs. 1200 should be purchased after it has been approved by the "Library Committee" of the respective circle or division. The library committee may consist of 3 to 4 members as may be decided by the Conservator or the Dy. Conservator of Forests.

(vi) **Selection after demand :** Some books may be required more by the readers and therefore more number of copies of such books should be purchased so that the no reader is deprived from issue of such books. This will also avoid bitterness amongst the library staff and the readers.

(vii) **Bibliographies :** The books to be purchased should also be selected from the bibliographies. A bibliography may be a closed one or a periodical one. Further a periodical bibliography may be (a) Indexing periodical, merely listing or bare entries of books such as catalogues supplied by various publishers, (b) Abstracting periodical giving an abstract at the end of each entry such as "Forestry abstract" which are regularly published by CAB International, United Kingdom.

(viii) **Readers Suggestion :** A suggestion book may be kept in the circle and division library to write their views and request for purchase of books, periodicals etc.

(ix) **T.A. for selection :** The budget should be provided for going to Dehradun and other places for the selection of library books.

The criteria or the method of selection or purchase of books is justified if there is at least one reader per book at some time or the other.

Resources in the Library

The major resources of the library include books, journals, reports, standards and patents. Each title should be selected by keeping in mind the library's immediate and long range objectives, the interest of the users, the present strength and weakness of its collection, its commitment for automatic receipt of materials, the size of the funds, co-operative agreements with other libraries, and library resources of other libraries in the immediate geographical area.

Before using the library, the reader should acquaint himself with the content structure of the scientific and technical literature published in the following three categories :

(1) **The Primary Resources** represent new knowledge and the most up to date information. These are the scientific periodicals, technical reports, conference proceedings, research-in-progress reports, reprints, commercial literature, patents, standards, theses / dissertations, publications of professional societies and government agencies.

(2) **The Secondary Sources** consist of republication of excerpts from primary sources. They exist in a variety of forms like books, journals, bibliographies, reference materials like databooks, dictionaries, handbooks, encyclopedias, tables, almanacs, statistical information, manuals, source book and how-to-do-it manuals, review serials and progress reviews.

(3) **The Tertiary Sources** are essentially aids to facilitate the use of both primary and secondary sources. They exist in the form of bibliography of bibliographies, directories, subject guides and general guides.

11

Book Order and Acquisition

Introduction

Once a book has been selected for purchase, an order has to be placed to acquire it. Placing book order requires a careful consideration of library organisation, staff, finance and procedures to be followed and the records to be maintained. The great variety and complex nature of documents to be acquired makes it necessary that order librarian should have good knowledge of bibliography, languages (English, local language, and Hindi) and scientific management. He should also know enough about book publishing and book selling trade.

The major problems that are faced by the forest libraries in the department are :

(i) Distances of leading book publishing centers are enormous and selection and procurement of books cause delay.

(ii) It is rather difficult to acquire publications from neighbouring countries due to inadequate trade facilities, restrictions on export (as foreign exchange is involved), bad relation between countries and lack of comprehensive up-to-date bibliographies.

(iii) Lack of funds.

(iv) Publications are frequently withdrawn from circulation due to political reasons.

(v) In our country, cash payment has to be made for government publications, which creates problems in purchasing books sold at government book shops.

Terms of Book Supply

The Good Offices Committee, New Delhi is a voluntary organization formed by the representatives of book trade and libraries to stabilize and introduce uniform terms of book and periodical supplies to libraries. The committee meets at regular intervals and after taking into consideration the fluctuations in currency rates decides the rates of conversion. It has also laid down discount rates for different categories of books and periodical publications as well as other terms for book supplies.

The terms of supply from the book seller should be made clear before placing the order.

Discounts

Many books carry discount of 10 per cent or even more, therefore before placing the order it must be ensured that the book seller/publisher will be making the bill after taking into account discount factor. Normally Central & State Government publications and journals and periodicals carry no discount.

Normally there is no necessity for calling quotations and tenders for purchase of scientific books and periodicals from Indian Vendors in India.

Before placing order for the purchase of books, make it sure that funds are available for the purpose. For items to be ordered, decide the vendor. Next type out three copies of the order-list. Send one copy with the order to Vendor. Second copy may be sent to the reference section. Third copy can be used as an office copy. On receiving the supply, tally the books and the bill. Determine whether the bill is in order. Tick mark the items received in the order file. Transmit the order slips with books and bill to the accession section. In case certain books are not supplied by the Vendor in expected time, then send reminders for the items not supplied.

If the book is out of print, then it may be useful to call for quotations from second-hand booksellers. By obtaining competitive quotation, a library would be able to save considerable amount especially for highly costly items.

A successful programme for the acquisition of documents requires a knowledge of publishers, of the book selling trade, and an understanding of the ordering policies, procedures, and practices. The order librarian should have bibliographical duplication either in the indent or in the order list. Sending of order lists is a work of-great responsibility. The libraries should follow the terms laid down by Good Offices Committee, New Delhi. These terms sensure a 'Fair working margin' to booksellers.

12

Accessioning

Introduction

After ordering the books are received along with the bills. The bills are checked with order list. The books are collated and tallied with bills. If books and bills are in order, then these alongwith corresponding book order slips are handed over to the staff member responsible for accessioning.

In the process of accessioning each volume added to the library receives a serial number in the order of acquisition to the library collection. This includes books purchased or received in exchange or as gift. This number is called accession number. Cumulated volumes of periodicals such as 'Indian Forester', which are to be bound and preserved in the library are also accessioned.

Accession number given to a volume is added in the order slip. Thus, at this stage, order slips become accession slips. Accession number is also recorded at the back of title page and on the conventional place of the volume. Accession number should also be written against the respective items in the bill for the purchased book. Then pass the bill for payment. File all the accession slips or cards in the sequence of their accession numbers in the *accession register cabinet*. In many libraries, accession slips are discarded after the books have been classified and catalogued and catalogue cards are filed in the public catalogue. They prefer to have a separate bound register called an accession register. An accession register constitutes records in which the books are accessioned.

The accession register and accession slips are official stock records of the library and must be kept under lock and key. The accession register and accession slips form the basic record of books and other documents of the library. This record gives a complete history of each book/periodical acquired by the library. When a book is withdrawn, then the corresponding accession slip is withdrawn or note regarding withdrawal is given in the accession register. In case a user loses a book then with the help of details given in the accession register, the user may be asked either to make payment or to replace the copy. If a library does not provide imprint and collation in the catalogue entries, then a reference librarian can provide this information from accession register or accession slips to a user, who requests for this information regarding a book on loan or misplaced.

The following is the form of *Accession Register*

Accession Register

Accession Number	*Date of accession*	*Author*	*Title*	*Edition*	*Publishers name & address*	*Year of Publication*
1	*2*	*3*	*4*	*5*	*6*	*7*

Pages & Volume No.	*Name of Supplier*	*Bill no. & Date*	*Price*	*Date of withdrawal*	*Re-marks*
8	*9*	*10*	*11*	*12*	*13*

13

Processing Work

The processing section of a library is the pivot around which all its activities revolve. The work of the processing is basic to other works of a library. Processing helps in the transformation of a collection of books into serviceable articles.

Classification

Classification is the foundation of librarianship. Classification in common parlance means arrangement and this "brings order out of chaos." In order to vouchsafe a permanent arrangement many classification schemes are in vogue. But for our library we shall be using the "Oxford system of Decimal Classification for Forestry."

Personnel

Classification work is not only a technical job but it needs sound subject background. Therefore in absence of trained librarian ACFs or RFOs should be entrusted with this work.

Classification Procedure

The books are received from the order section after accessioning. The following jobs are performed for classifying the books :—

(i) **Determining the specific subject** : The books to be put for cataloguing requires the following informations :—

Title, sub-title, foreword, preface, Table of contents, Book Jackets, flaps and book reviews.

Generally the specific subject can be found out by reading the title of a book but in cases where the specific subject is not clear from the title because of its misleading nature, the other parts of the book as given above are gone through.

(ii) **Allotting class numbers** : After determining the subject of each book, the classification schedule is used for allotting proper class numbers. It should be made clear whether close or broad classification is to be practiced in the library otherwise there will be a lot of confusion. For forest libraries the broad classification would be sufficient. The class numbers should first be given in pencil so that after rechecking it may be corrected.

Cataloguing

Classification determines the place of a book on the shelves. Physically book can be placed only at one place according to the subject contents of the book. But the readers seek book through various approaches such as author, title, series, and other collaborators like translators, editors etc. Classification is not capable of fulfilling these varied approaches of the readers. The catalogue comes to the *rescue* of the readers. As a city without a map is difficult to be known about, so is a library without a catalogue.

The cataloguing should be done by a sincere person otherwise cataloguing instead of serving as a guide will become a hindrance. The help of an experienced librarian should be taken for this. The catalogue should be typed by a good typist. In experienced and raw hands should not be engaged for cataloguing.

Kinds of Catalogues

There are many kinds of catalogues. The catalogue can be either simplified or descriptive, similarly it can be classified catalogue or Dictionary type of catalogue. The Dictionary catalogues are convenient to the readers. Again it is to be decided as to whether a typed, hand-written or a printed catalogue is to be maintained. For the forestry library "typed card catalogue" should be used.

Cataloguing Procedure

The cataloguing of books is an arduous job. It must be planned intelligently if it has to serve its purpose. The following are the jobs involved in cataloguing —

(i) **Preparation of main entry :** In accordance with the rules of the cataloguing code in use, one of the cataloguers prepares the main entry card. This main entry card contains maximum information about the book on the back side in pencil so that it can be changed without any damage to the card. By writing it on the back of the card, the readers are also saved from unnecessary confusion.

(ii) **Preparation of Shelf list :** A shelf list card is a duplicate copy of the main entry card. For each book, one shelf list card is prepared.

(iii) **Preparation of added and reference entries :** Preparation of a main entry is a responsible job and the other added entries are merely duplication of the main entry with minor alterations and / or deletions etc. So it is better if this repetitive job is assigned, to junior staff members. The tracings on the back of the main entry card provide instructions to the juniors for preparing added and reference entries without any difficulty.

(iv) **Label pasting** : After the preparation of catalogue cards the books are given to unskilled worker for pasting labels in the books.

(a) **Spine label :** Gummed white cloth is cut into round or square pieces of about 1.25″ each. This label is pasted one inch above the bottom of the spine of the book. This is done to facilitate "call Number" to be visible to the readers when the book is shelved in a book rack.

Class No.
Book No.

(b) **Ownership slip/mark :** One ownership slip is generally pasted on the inner side of the front card board at left hand top most corner. The size of this slip may be about 3″ x 2.5″. The slip may be made of glazed paper. The specimen of the slip is given below —

Name of the Library
Class No.........................
Book No.........................
Acc. No...........................

(c) **Ownership stamp** : The other ownership marks are put at various places of the book by rubber stamps or embossing machines. A stamp which contains the name of the library is put on the title page and another on the secret page, to be decided by each library. Third stamp may be put at the end of the book. The specimen of ownership stamp is as under :—

Name of the Library

....

Location/Place ....

(d) **Date slip :** One date slip is pasted on the top most portion of the front or back fly-leaf of each book. But for reference books, manuscripts and other books which are not to be issued, this slip is not pasted. The size of the slip is 5″ x 3″ with the following specimen—

Call No.		Name of the library		Acc. No.	
Date		Date		Date	
Issue	Return	Issue	Return	Issue	Return

(e) **Book pocket :** On the bottom of the inner right side of the front or back card-board cover, a book pocket of 5″ x 3″ size is pasted. Its specimen is given below :—

Book Pocket

Open flap

Name of the Library ....

Brief Library Rules ....

(f) **Book card :** One printed book card of 5″ x 3″ size is put in the book pocket of each book. But in case of reference and other non-issuable books, this card is not slipped in the book pocket. The specimen of this card is given below:—

Book Card

Call No. .... Acc. No. ....

Name of Library ....

Author ....

Title ....

Name	issue date	Return date

(v) Label writing and assigning location marks : The pasted labels are written in ink. Superior type of ink and nibs are used for this repetitive job. But this job is very important one because if the labels are not accurately written, the book is likely to be misplaced. The spine labels contain the call number and the location mark of the book. These words are abbreviated and followed consistently. The specimens are given below :

Rare 025 S 10 D	R 025 W 10 D	RR 025 W 10 D
For rare book	For Reference Book.	For Report used as a Reference Book.

(vi) Catalogue cards checking by chief cataloguer : All the cards alongwith the catalogued books are submitted to the chief cataloguer for scrutiny and checking. The mistakes are corrected. It is better if the books are sent to the librarian for further checking. The books are thus ready to be shelved and the catalogue cards are ready to be filed in the catalogue and shelf list cabinets.

(vii) Alphabetization : The catalogue cards to be filed in the catalogue are alphabetized. For alphabetizing, there are two accepted methods *i. e.* word by word or letter by letter. The shelf list cards are arranged in a classified order.

(viii) **Card filing :** The shelf list cards are merged in the shelf list. Other catalogue cards are merged in the public catalogues. Due to many kinds of entries it is to be decided as to which cards are to be filed first. Whether the arrangement should be by author, subject, title, series etc.? or it should be by subject, author, title, series etc. It is better if a particular code is followed for this purpose. "A.L.A. filing rules" should be followed for filing catalogue cards if some other rules are not being followed.

(ix) **Authority file :** The authority file contains the complete information about the adopted names of authors and subject heading. In this way consistency and uniformity are maintained.

(x) **Preparation of list of additions** : Every good library publishes periodically a list of additions. It is list of books added to the library from time to time. Its main purpose is to inform the readers about the reading material acquired by the library.

For our purpose cyclostyled list of additions in the month of December and June would be appropriate under the title "Library News."

14

Maintenance Work

The importance of the maintenance of a library needs no emphasis. If proper care is not taken to organise and administer it on sound lines, the library property would become unserviceable in no time. It should be continuously watched that books are correctly shelved on the book racks.

Staking

In order to ensure an efficient and economical scheme it is necessary, when planning a stacking scheme that :

(a) Wastage of space should be avoided to as much extent as possible.

(b) Maximum number of books should be shelved in minimum amount of space.

(c) The shelves should be as much attractive, functional and durable as possible.

The standard racks or shelves are made of teak, shisham or steel.

The steel racks are manufactured by —

(1) M/s. Godrej Co., Bombay.

(2) M/s. J.K.S. Company, Hubli.

(3) M/s. Siddeshwar & Co. Pvt. Ltd., Hubli.

(4) Decor Steel Pvt. Ltd., New Delhi and Chandigarh.

(5) M/s. Vinar Limited, Delhi.

Shelving Methods

The books may be classified alphabetically, chronologically or systematically by subject as circumstances may control or suggest.

(i) **Classified arrangement** : One method which is commonly used by most of the libraries is the arrangement of books in a classified manner i.e. in the order, of a classification scheme (here Oxford system) used in the library. If Decimal classification is used then the arrangement of books will be as under :

000	100	200	300	400
500	600	700	800	900

So far as is practicable the stock should be arranged in unbroken sequence upon the shelves, but exceptions have sometimes to be allowed. For physical reasons it is frequently found necessary to have 'size grouping' of books.

(ii) **Broken order** : Some books are in great demand while others may not be used by the readers very frequently. The time of the readers is to be saved and efforts are to be made to ensure that all requisite books are brought to the notice of the readers. Reference books, text books, children's book etc. are placed separately because these would be accessible easily if these are arranged in special sequences. All this implies a broken order in which the arrangement of books is not strictly in accordance with the classified order.

This broken order may be as under :

800	920	320	—
Ref. books	Juvenile books	100	200
300	400	500	600
700	—	—	—

(iii) **Parallel arrangement** : If the books are arranged in a classified manner and by size, a system of parallel order may be followed. It means that books of various sizes on a particular subject are arranged on the same shelves in such a manner that no space is wasted and books are made available without any extra labour. Books of smaller sizes on a particular subject may be arranged behind the books of normal size. The books of abnormal sizes may be arranged on the lower most shelf.

In forest office the classified arrangement will be suitable and convenient.

Shelving special books and non-book materials

Reports of Seminar, Bulletins, maps, Atlases, dictionary etc. should be stacked separately.

Tools for proper functioning of the maintenance

For proper maintenance the following articles should be provided :

(i) **Book ends or Book supports** : These should be provided in large numbers. At least two book supports are required for one plank so that the books are made to stand erect.

(ii) **Book trolly** : To carry books from one end to the other end book-trolly should be used.

(iii) **Shelving tables** : One small table for sorting out books for shelving should be provided in each bay of stacks.

(iv) **Guide boards** : The guide boards will facilitate the readers to locate the books in the shelves. The readers will get overall view of the arrangement of books on the shelves.

Open Access Vs. Closed Access

In open access libraries there always remains a danger of mutilation and damage of books by unscrupulous readers. But the readers have got the liberty to consult the books and in this manner, they can select their appropriate reading materials. It eliminates as many barriers between the books and readers as possible. Their valuable time is also saved. Their time is liable to be wasted in closed access system in which a reader by consulting the catalogue gives a requisition slip and he gets the books issued for home reading. But on perusing the book, he may find that it does not serve his purpose. He returns the book on the next day and selects another book by consulting the catalogue. From the safety point of view it is advisable to follow the closed access system.

15

Periodical Work

Introduction

A periodical publication consists of periodicals (including indexing and abstracting periodicals) and serials. Bulk of primary source literature appears in the form of periodicals. The periodical article is the main means of communication for the exchange of scientific information. Information contained in periodicals is almost invariably more up to date than that appearing in books. Periodicals usually report the results of recent researches more quickly than books. The experience has shown that most of the material reported in periodicals is never published in books. Therefore the libraries are expected to maintain long files of back volumes of periodicals such as that of " The Indian Forester", "Journal of Indian Forestry", "My Forest" etc.

Magazines, periodicals and journals are published at various intervals. The frequency of their publication may be daily, bi-weekly, fortnightly, monthly, bi-monthly, quarterly, half-yearly, annual or irregular.

Selection of Periodicals and Serials

The selection of forestry periodicals should not be left in one or two hands but like as for the books there must be a committee for this purpose so that judicious selection may be made possible. The general principles of periodical selection do not vary essentially from those governing the selection of books. The factors governing selection depend on :

(i) The financial resources of the library,

(ii) Periodicals already taken,

(iii) The scope of the library,

(iv) Demand of readers.

Ordering

The current periodicals are acquired by the following means :

(a) Subscription orders, (b) membership of professional societies, (c) Exchange, and (d) gift. The greater number are acquired through subscription orders. A few can be received through membership.

At the time of making order mention complete bibliographical details for the periodical, giving title, name of the publisher/ distributor, volume number and year. Always request for the bill in triplicate. Indicate whether it should be mailed by surface mail or by air mail.

The periodical order work involves the following jobs :

1. New periodicals ordering,
2. Renewals ordering,
3. Backsets of periodicals ordering.

Recording the Receipt of Periodicals

The two kinds of system may be followed :

(i) **Register system** : The periodicals may be entered in an alphabetical manner or according to their frequency of publication. One page may be used for recording many periodicals. As soon as the issue of a periodical is received, the date of its receipt is entered in the month column against the periodical in question and similarly date is put on the title cover of the periodical. An ownership stamp is also put on the title cover.

(ii) **Ledger system** : The periodical publications subscribed may be entered in a permanent ledger in an alphabetical or numerical order and an index of the periodicals subscribed is given in the beginning of the ledger.

Display

All the periodicals should be registered promptly and sent for display. These should be displayed on display shelves of periodical display rack. Preceding issues should be replaced by the current ones.

Issue

The periodicals should not be issued to the members, however, the photocopy of the article may be given to the reader.

16

Circulation Work

Introduction

The books are displayed on the shelves and a 'reference desk' is provided so that readers may get guidance for selecting their reading material. The books may be used within the library premises but all persons who are animated with the desire of reading may not be able to find out so much spare time that they are able to sit in the library for reading purposes. The question arises as to how the library resources can be utilized properly. Are the books to be preserved? In fact, the circulation of books for home use is the major service by the library. The best equipped library located in the most modern plant and staffed with the most capable librarians would be a mausoleum of recorded knowledge if the circulation function is omitted. The circulation brings in productive relationship between users and library materials. The various methods for this will be discussed under the topic "charging and discharging methods." The circulation work for forestry library should involve the following jobs :

1. Registration of members,
2. Lending of Books,
3. Charging of overdues,
4. Reservation of books,
5. Renewal of books,
6. Overnight issues,

7. Maintenance of records,
8. Miscellaneous jobs.

1. **Registration of members** : The books should be allowed for taking home only to the registered members. The person who wants to be registered will fill up a membership form which will contain following details :

Name, post, present local address, permanent address, name and signature of the guarantor (who will already be a registered member).

This application will be addressed to the library incharge in forest office. The application forms should be in a tray alphabetically. The reverse side of the card will contain following informations:

Amount deposited, particulars checked and found in order.

The fees should be charged, from every member.

Each member should be allotted a membership number. Only the persons serving in that division or circle should be made member. This will avoid many problems while dealing with the members.

After a person is enrolled as a member, he will be given a membership card or membership-cum-identity card. On this card any two books will be issued at one time.

2. **Lending of books** : On the membership card any two books will be issued at one time.

(a) **Charging procedure** : The member will select the book and take them to the issue counter alongwith his card. The issuing clerk after following the charging procedure duly will issue the book.

(b) **Discharging procedure** : The member after reading the books will come back to the library for returning the books. He will present the books at the counter. The cards of books alongwith the membership card will be taken out from the tray, the book cards (both) will be slipped into the book pockets and membership card will be returned back to the member. The issuing clerk will ensure that late-fees have been charged from the member.

3. **Charging of overdues** : The books returned after due date will be accepted after taking late-fees or overdue charges. If he does not deposit the overdue his membership will be cancelled. The

overdue may be charged at an uniform rate of say Rs. 2 per week. A receipt will be given by the issuing clerk.

4. **Reservation of Books**: Many books remain in great demand. When readers or members find some difficulty in getting particular book in a library they can apply for the reservation of book on a piece of paper and the librarian will inform him by post or in person that the book has become available for issue.

5. **Renewal of Books** : Some important books are required by readers time after again, because they may require it constantly or that the book being lengthy may require more time for studying them thoroughly. Such book may be reissued to the same member when that book is not in demand. But care must be taken to ensure that the demand of the reader is genuine. In other words the book should not be renewed at the expense of other genuine readers.

6. **Overnight issues** : There may be certain books whose issue is to be restricted because these are required in the library at any time. But because books are to be put to maximum use and every reader is to be given his requisite book, it is proper to devise a method by which the readers may be enabled to read the required books. This method is known as 'Overnight issue of books'. In this method books are issued at the time of closing the library and the readers are asked to return the books within an hour of the opening of the library on the next day. The condition for the issue of such books is that if it is not returned within the stipulated period a special overdue charge at the enhanced rate may be charged and he will not be issued other book on his membership card till then.

7. **Maintenance of Records** : The maintenance of circulation records is very important because these become the sound basis for preparing various comparative statements. It has been discussed in detail in the chapter "Library Records".

8. **Miscellaneous Jobs** : The other jobs which are involved in the circulation selection include the following :

(a) Issue of reminders/recovery of over-due books,

(b) Replacement of lost library books/cards,

(c) Replacement of lost membership card,

(d) Provision of safety measures,

(e) Issue of clearance certificates.

17

Charging and Discharging Methods

Introduction

The books are acquired, processed and kept in libraries for use. These are written not for their own sake but to enlighten the readers. Their destination is the readers hand. The books can be either used within the library premises or at home. Most of the readers like to take the books for home-reading. The method used for issue and return of books is called 'charging system' or 'circulation control system'. Charging systems exist in a great variety. Two main kinds of popular charging systems are (1) Ledger system and (2) Card system.

The choice of charging system should be such as to provide the following answers :

(i) Who has borrowed a particular volume on loan ? When it is due ?

(ii) Which and how many books subject-wise have been borrowed on any date?

(iii) How many books were returned on any date ?

The charging system to be chosen should be the one which takes least possible time in issue and return of books. It should also be economical in terms of staff, money and materials. The following two kinds of system may be followed—(I) Browne's system or (II) Ledger system.

(I) **Browne's card issue system** : This system was devised by Nile E. Browne who was librarian of the Library Bureau in Bostan and served as the Secretary of the Publishing Board of the American Library Association. This system should be used in our forest libraries.

(i) Requisite materials

(a) For the book :

1. Date slip

One 5" x 3" slip is pasted opposite to the page facing the card-board back/front cover of the book in the following form :

Name of the library ....

Call No.....................Accession No.................................

The following books were issued/are due on the below mentioned dates.

Date of issue	Due date	Date of issue	Due date

2. Book Pocket

One 5" x 3" book pocket is pasted on the inside back/front cover card board of the book.

3. Book Card

One 4" x 2" book card is prepared for each book and is inserted inside the book pocket of the book. This card contains :

Call No........................... Acc No. ....

Author ....

Title ....

(b) For the borrowers :

1. **Borrower's tickets or pockets** : Each borower is given as many tickets (two in this case) which are in the form of pockets of tough paper as he is entitled to borrow books. This ticket (in the shape of pocket) is of size 3" x 2". It opens on two sides i.e. the upper and the left or right portions. This pocket contains the name and address of the borrower, the date of expiry of membership, the signature and stamp of the Librarian. On the back of it, the seal of the library is printed.

(c) For the Counter Staff

1. Registration no. and membership card of the borrower.
2. Date stamp and Ink pad.
3. Charging trays of steel or wood of 1' x 12' size with four drawers.
4. Stationery articles including pencils, printed lined sheets for circulation statistics, reminder cards and reservation cards.

Charging

The reader will surrender as many Reader's Tickets to the counter Assistant as he wants to get the books issued. The Counter Assistant after identifying the reader will take out the book card from the book pocket of the book and will slip the book card in the Reader's pocket and will stamp either date of issue or due date as the case may be on the date slip and will hand over the book to the reader. The book card and the reader's pocket together are filed in the charging tray.

Discharging Procedure

There are two types of discharging procedure :

I. Book Card System :

When the user returns the book, the book card is located by means of date on the date label and other book identification details. If the book is overdue, the fine will be charged at the rate of say 25 paisa per day or Rs. 2 per week. The reader's ticket is given to the user and book card is inserted in blank pocket.

The following is the form of Borrowers ticket of size 4" x 3".

Name of Library ....

Borrower's Name ....

Address ....

Registration No. ....

Signature of the Borrower .

II. Ledger System :

In this system the ledger to be maintained consists of numbered pages. One page is allotted to each borrower as below :

Name of borrower ....

Registration No. ....

S.No.	Date of issue	Author	Title of book	Date of return	Librarian's Signature

The ledger system can be started initially and after the library runs in full swing then only Browne's system should be adoped.

18

Library Rules and Regulations

Introduction

If an organisation is to be run successfully and efficiently it requires certain principles. These principles or rules and regulations must be followed by its members so that the desired results may be achieved without any hindrance. The rules lay down the privileges and duties of the members of an organisation so that they may know their limits precisely and there may not be any confusion. The libraries and books are meant for use and if no rules are laid down, the books instead of being put to proper use, may be misused and this may kill the very purpose of the libraries.

Rules of the Library

The library rules should be few, simple, flexible and plausible. The language of the rules should be expressive and legalistic. Flexibility in rules is essential for the reason that an organisation frames certain rules to facilitate its working. In fact, rules are a means to serve an end. The rules should not become the master, but should remain the servants of an institution so that the Librarian should have discretion to mould the rules in certain urgent situations. The following rules are being prescribed for the departmental libraries :

1. Name of the Library ....

2. Working hours : The library shall remain open to the members on all working days during office hours except on National & Gazetted holidays.

The issue counter will be closed half an hour before the closing hours.

3. Admission to the Library :

(i) All persons may be allowed admission in the library but admission may be refused if a person is shabily dressed or is intoxicated.

(ii) Every person who enters the library shall sign the 'Gate Register'.

(iii) All personal belongings except purses and note-books shall not be allowed to be carried with the readers beyond the issue counter. These shall be deposited at the property counter.

(iv) Pets such as dogs, cats, etc. shall not be admitted to the library.

(v) The readers shall keep pin drop silence within the Library

(vi) No reader is allowed to sleep in the library premises.

(vii) Tea, coffee, snacks etc. are not allowed in the library.

(viii) Smoking is strictly prohibited in the library.

4. General

(i) The librarian may refuse to loan books to any person without assigning any reason or may grant special permission to any person to use the library.

(ii) The readers shall behave in a civilized manner. The Librarian may expel any person if the presence of such a person is liable to create law and order situation.

(iii) The readers are liable for punishment or fine if they either misbehave or damage the books or any other property of the library.

Circulation Control System

(i) Every employee working in the division or circle may be eligible for the membership.

(ii) Each prospective member shall give in writing an undertaking to abide by the rules of the library. He shall fill up a 'membership form' available at the circulation counter, after which he/she will be provided with Reader's Ticket.

(iii) Every member shall be provided with a Reader's Ticket.

(iv) Every member shall present his Reader's Ticket before any book or journal is issued to him. Normally maximum number of four books and four reports can be issued to a member at a time.

(v) In case of loss of Reader's Ticket, the matter shall be reported to the librarian and if the librarian is satisfied a new Reader's Ticket will be issued after recovery price of the new card say Rs. 5/-. The member will be responsible for any misuse of lost Reader's Ticket.

(vi) The books shall be issued to the borrower for a fortnight. In special cases the books may be issued for a month.

(vii) The members shall not sub-lent the books issued from the library. The borrower should not make notes on, underline in, tear off pages, damage or mutilate the publications borrowed by him/her.

(viii) If the books are not returned on the due date an overdue charge at the rate of say 25 paisa per book per day or Rs. 2 per week per book shall be charged for extra days for which the books have been kept.

(ix) In case any book is lost or injured by the member, the member shall replace the book or shall pay the cost of replacement. If the library is not in a position to procure a new copy of the book for replacement for any reason, the borrower will be asked to pay 3 times the cost of the book. Photocopy will not be accepted as replacement of the book.

(x) Reference books, rare-books, unbound periodicals and current issues of journals may not be issued generally except with the permission of the head of office. In special cases, such books and journals may be issued for a maximum period of Two hours against the Reader's Tickets. Only those bound volumes which are five years or more old will be issued. The loan period for each volume shall not exceed one week.

(xi) The books may be renewed for the further period if the same are not in demand or are not reserved by other readers. The renewal will be done generally on the physical presentation of the books.

(xii) If a member does not pay off the library dues, the privilege of borrowing books may be suspended till he deposits the requisite amount.

(xiii) The librarian shall have the power to refuse the issue of a book to any member or he may recall any book without assigning any reason therefor.

(xiv) Any material which is on loan could be reserved.

(xv) All the publications borrowed should be returned before going on deputation or leave exceeding one month.

19

Stock Verification and Shelf Rectification

Introduction

Stock verification implies the physical check-up of the articles on record. If some books are lost, due to variety of reasons, it is essential to replace them so that no gap is created in the usual library services. This would be possible only if periodical physical check up of the library stock is made. Though, theoretically it may not be very essential to resort to regular stock-taking yet in practice, it is both essential and desirable to have some kind of checking so that inherent defects in the administrative policies may be detected and possible remedies may be devised to eradicate these maladies.

From the professional point of view stock-verification should not be equated with physical verification of stock. It is also concerned with 'Maintenance and shelf rectification of stock'. The books may be lost, mutilated and misplaced. Lost books should be written off if the responsibility can not be fixed for the loss. The damaged books would have to be repaired. In case too many books are found to have been lost, mutilated and misplaced, then steps would have to be taken to improve the situation.

The aims of stock verification are :

(i) To prepare the list of lost books,

(ii) To find out misplaced books and take them out for current placing,

(iii) Determine the physical conditions of the books and locate those requiring repair,

(iv) To locate books requiring correction work and those which can be discarded.

Methods of Verification : The following methods can be used for stock verification:

(i) By accession register,

(ii) By using a separate register with Accession numbers,

(iii) By preparing separate sheets which contain accession numbers in a consecutive order,

(iv) Stock-taking by numerical counting,

(v) By book cards or Duplicate set of Book-cards.

(i) **By accession register** : The accession number is taken to the shelves and one person calls the particulars of books from the shelf alongwith the Accession Number and the other person ticks the concerned Accession Number in the Accession register. When all the books are checked, a list of untraceable items is prepared and efforts are made to trace out the missing books. This method is time consuming and rather cumbersome. It leads to spoiling of the accession register.

(ii) **By using a separate register with Accession Number** : In this method a separate stock-taking register is prepared with the following columns :

Accession No.	*1989*	*1990*	*1991*	*1992*	*1993*	*Remarks*
1						
2						
3						
4						
5						
6						
7						

The register is taken to the shelves. The person calls out the accession number from the book, another person tick marks the relevant column against the particular accession number. At the end of stock taking, a list is prepared on separate sheets, tracing of the untraceable books is done and the items found afterwards either from the Issue records or Binding section or from the shelves are, crossed from this list. This is a time consuming method and is not recommended for large libraries. Here only two persons can do stock verification at a time. This is a great handicap.

(iii) Loose sheets listing accession number : In order to obviate the necessity of getting printed the new "stocktaking register" after some years or of preparing fresh accession numbers, a new and simple method can be used for stock verification by preparing separate sheets which have Accession numbers upto the last item acquired in the library. A single sheet may contain 100 accession numbers. Multiple copies can be produced so that many persons can do stock verification at a time. An accession number called out is crossed out in the sheet. The numbers which have not been crossed represent untraceable books. This method is better than the use of register listing Accession Numbers. It takes less time.

(iv) Numerical Counting of Books : This involves merely counting of books lying on shelves and those on loan. This number if deducted out of total stock based on accession register would lead to the number of books lost. On knowing the average cost of a book, one can calculate the cost of lost books. This system however does not serve the basic purposes for which stock taking practice has been started.

(v) By book cards or duplicate set of book cards : The book cards are taken out from book pockets. These are arranged accession number-wise. Thus a list of missing numbers is prepared. List of missing books is compiled with the help of accession register. In this method handling of large number of books may become a problem and book cards can also get misplaced. Later these are arranged by call number and put back in the book pockets.

Similarly duplicate book cards of different colours are prepared at the time of processing of books. At the time of stock-taking the book cards are exchanged from the catalogue cabinet to the books. The cards of the particular colour which remain in the catalogue cabinet indicate the loss of books after ascertaining the books which are issued or have been withdrawn already or have been sent for binding. This system also entails lot of work and time.

Frequency of Stock Verification

The stock verification in the Dy. C.F. and C.F. libraries should be carried out once in every year. Regions of shelves which are more prone to loss of books should be subjected to more frequent stock verification. The stock verification should be completed within 20 days in the month of June and during this period the library should be closed for the readers.

Shelf List or Register

In a library there would be a number of sequences of collections. In order to control the movement of books we make use of a shelf list. This does not apply to the movement of books when these are taken from the shelf and get into the hands of the users. A shelf list consists of cards of standard size 7.5 cm. x 12.5 cm. A library may use catalogue cards without lines or coloured cards for this purpose. These cards are arranged in a classified order. For each volume there would be one card. Shelf cards are kept parallel and move parallel to corresponding books on the shelves. If a book is transferred from one sequence to another one, then its shelf card would also be shifted. Shelf list enables the library to maintain correct sequence on the shelves and to put every book in the correct place. It can also indicate immediately the position of any book on the shelf in the library.

Shelf Rectification

At the time of borrowing and returning, the books are liable to be misplaced. This would require restoration of order. The process of restoring order among the books is called 'shelf-rectification'.

Care and Repair of Books

Books are the life-blood of great thinkers of the past and the present. They represent life-long labours, researches and studies undertaken. Therefore it is our religious duty to conserve this knowledge in an appropriate manner. Books like human beings have got a body and a soul.

The following are the five enemies of the books :

1. Insects 2. Water 3. Fire 4. Dust and 5. Human beings.

1. **Insects** : Some insects are sworn enemies of books. These insects include cockroaches, white-ants, mold or mildew, silver fish and beetles.

The control measures include use of gammaxene, B.H.C., thimet, D.D.T., Napthalene balls etc.

The white ants should be destroyed alongwith the queen. Steel furniture and concrete buildings should be used for storing books. The cracks and crevices in the building should be treated with B.H.C., thimet or with some other insecticide.

2. **Water** : Water or humidity is harmful for the books. Use of air-conditioning helps to maintain the desired level of temperature and humidity. It increases the life of the reading material. Books attacked by fungus should be cleaned individually.

3. **Fire** : Fire can destroy all the books. Too much sunlight is also not good for the books. Library should be provided with fire extinguisher and fire buckets.

4. **Dust** : The libraries should be made dust free in a suitable manner. Dust is the direct cause of insect breeding.

5. **Human beings** : Some human beings are prone to antisocial habit of stealing and mutilating books. Therefore these habits should be discouraged by suitable devices.

20

Library Records

Classification of Records

The records to be maintained in a library can be classified as below :

(i) Records of books and other non-book resources available in the library,

(ii) Cost records i.e. total cost and unit cost etc.,

(iii) Service records i.e. services rendered by the library, and

(iv) Administrative records.

(i) Record of books and other non-book materials

(a) **Record of books :** The record of books is directly connected with the expenditure made on purchase of books . For this an "Accession Register" should be made containing the following details :—

Date, Accession No., Author, Title, Publisher and Name of Publication, Price, Volume, Source of supply, Bill No., Date and Amount, Call No., Remarks.

(b) **Record of non-book materials** : For non-book reading materials i.e. maps, charts, microfilms, atlas etc. a type of "Accession Register" should be made but additional columns for detailed information about the script, format and other Physical aspects should be provided which are not found in the records of reading materials in the book form. It is advisable to maintain separate registers for non-book materials since their purpose, use, handling and location etc. will otherwise bring in so many difficulties.

The records of these non-book materials should also be placed on cards.

(c) **Account Books** : This pertains to the acquisition of books etc. and preserving the relevant bills. The double payment should not be made. The bill register should contain the following details - Sr. No., Bill No. and Date, Name of Supplier, Amount of Bill, Deduction if any, Date of passing and Remarks.

(d) **Bill Files** : The bills should be kept supplier-wise. The files should be kept in vertical file-cabinets in an alphabetical order.

(e) **Shelf list** : The shelf list can be maintained in two ways.

(1) In the register form

(2) In the card form. The cards are kept in cabinets and are arranged in a classified order. The utility of this record lies in the fact that it can show the position of any book on the shelves. The shelf list is the most handy and time-saving tool for stock-verification purposes since each card represents exactly each book in the same position as it is to be found on the shelves.

(f) **Book Catalogue** : It helps the readers in finding out the required materials. Three types of cards for each book will be maintained,

(1) According to serial no. of classification i.e. class no.

(2) According to Author (A/Z).

(3) According to Title (A/Z).

In fact for every book five cards should be made, three cards for cataloguing and the remaining two for use at the time of issue of the book. These two additional cards will remain attached to the end of book.

(g) **Technical Records** : Such records pertain to the practices that have been followed in classification and cataloguing procedures. Here we shall be maintaining the record of "OXFORD SYSTEM OF DECIMAL CLASSIFICATION FOR FORESTRY". For non-forestry books system of accession number may be followed.

(ii) **Cost Records** : The cost records include the total amount spent on staff, book purchase etc. In short the cost records reveal the total cost of providing library service during a particular period by taking into account all the amounts spent from the moment the books are selected to the time these are actually made available to the readers.

From these records, we can arrive at the unit cost through cost-accounting process. These records should be kept under the following heads :

1. Salaries and Wages,
2. Purchase of books and other reading materials,
3. Library binding etc,
4. Maintenance charges,
5. Miscellaneous.

(iii) **Service records**

(a) **Visitor's Register**: A visitor's register in a library is essential to know the names and number of interested readers so that it can be judged whether the staff or community is utilizing the library properly or not. The visitor's register shall contain the following details :

Date, Sr. No., Name of Visitor, Designation and Address, Signature, Remarks.

(b) **Issue Records** : These records are to be maintained by the lending section at the issue counter. The following records are to be maintained.

Members record	—	The names and addresses of the members or readers.
Book record	—	The clue giving information about books issued.

For this purpose two cards can also be used, one card will go in the members cabinet and the other will go in the issue cabinet.

(c) **Time Record** : The Dy. C.F. or C.F. concerned will put a time limit (which may be different for textbooks and reference books etc.) for keeping the books for home use so that every reader gets a chance to make use of the books.

(d) **Overdues Record** : It is allied to time record. The names of the defaulters are noted in this record.

(iv) **Administrative Records** : The following records should be maintained.

(a) **Duties allocation chart** : This will contain the duty hours and nature of duties allotted to the men working in the library.

(b) **Leave Register** : This will reveal the names of the persons who go on leave.

21

Statistics and Annual Report

Introduction

Statistics refers to the method of dealing with quantitative information, involving collection, presentation, analysis and interpretation. The head of the department would like to know—'How well the library is doing ?' The comparison of statistics over a few years can indicate the position of the library.

The librarian can use statistics for the following purposes :

(a) To compile the annual report,

(b) To measure efficiency of different sections or individuals,

(c) On the basis of statistics, a new service can be planned or an existing service can be improved. The statistics will indicate whether there is likely to be enough demand for the new service,

(d) To prepare a case for increase in funds and staff,

(e) To present to users and higher authorities the achievements of the library.

The following statistics may be collected about the Forest-libraries :

(i) **Acquisition** : Number of documents obtained subjectwise by purchase, gift, exchange or membership.

(ii) **Classification** : Number of different types of documents classified according to subject.

(iii) **Cataloguing** : Number of documents catalogued and number of cards prepared.

(iv) **Membership** : Number of members in each rank. Number of members and non-members, who visited the library.

(v) **Issue** : Number of books and other documents issued. The issue statistics may be gathered language-wise, user-wise, category of document-wise, subject-wise etc.

(vi) **Reference service** : Number of queries in terms of ready and long range reference service. Number of queries which could not be answered.

(vii) **Periodicals** : Statistics regarding periodicals should be maintained separately which should be based on the frequency of publications.

(viii) **Staff** : Figures about incoming and outgoing staff.

(ix) **Expenditure** : The figures of expenditure on various items.

(x) **Income** : This includes income by way of membership and disposal of unwanted stock.

The statistics should be presented in the form of tables. The forms to be used must be simple, clear and attractive.

Annual Report

An annual report is the survey of the actual work done during the preceding year. It differs from a budget as the latter is an estimate for the coming year while the former is the medium through which we can know the progress or regress of various divisions and circles during the previous year. An annual report is, perhaps the best medium through which the achievements and shortcomings of the library may be seen and bottlenecks may be removed for improvement.

The annual report should cover the following heads :

(i) Clientele or users,

(ii) Book stock,

(iii) Services-Classification, Cataloguing and documentation,

(iv) Extension services or reprography,

(v) Staff,

(vi) Finance - expenditure and income,

(vii) Miscellaneous.

Proforma for Annual Report

For the year ....

A. General

1. Name of Library ....
2. Date of Establishment ....
3. Working hours ....
4. No. of days closed in the year ....

B. Clientele or Users

1. Total number of members. ....

CCF	CF	Dy.CF	ACF	RFO	FR.	FG	NGOs	Others	Total
___	___	___	___	___	___	___	___	___	___

2. New members added during the year ....
3. Ratio of members to the total staff in the Division/Circle ....

C. *Book Stock*

Books, Periodicals, *Newspapers etc.*

Indian / Foreign

1. Total no. of volumes at the year beginning ....
2. No. of volumes added ....
3. Total no. of volumes at the close of year. ....

D. *Services*

1. Whether the book stock is classified or not..................
2. Classification scheme in use ....
3. Physical form of the catalogue ....
   - (a) Card/book/shelf..............................
   - (b) Manuscript/typed/printed..............................
4. Total books issued and returned ....
5. Average no. of books issued daily ....
6. No. of books consulted daily..............................
7. No. of enquiries received..............................

E. *Staff*

No. of employees...

ACF	RFO	Fr.	Accountant	Clerk	Total
......	......	......	....	....	....

F. *Indexing and Abstracting*

1. No. of indexes made ....
2. No. of periodical articles abstracted ....

G. *Finance*

1. Recurring ....
2. Non-recurring ....

Total = ...

3. Revenue ....

H. *Cost Accounting*

1. Cost of service per book ....
2. Cost of service per reader ....
3. Budget provision per reader ....

I. *Miscellaneous.*

General observations about library.

Signature of Reporting Authority

22

Library Building and Facilities

A right type of planning is vital to the efficient working of a library. Planning of a library building requires thorough understanding of needs of the users, objectives and functions of a library. Mistakes made at this stage could prove to be extremely serious. A library planned for close access system would be unsuitable for open access system. But a library planned for open access is suitable for close access also. Till now the library planning in the forest department has been somewhat casual. However, there is beginning to be an increasing realization that this is an important job and should be carried out rather seriously.

A. Requirement of Library building

The following are the general requirements of a library building :—

(i) **Functional** : A library building should have functional design rather than a monumental one. The factors which are intrinsically important in a good library such as functionality and expansibility should be given importance. The present libraries in the forest offices are not functional.

(ii) **Open access** : A library building designed for 'Open access system' is also considered useful for a 'close access system'. But it is not true vice-versa. Provision of 'Open access system' has certain implications'. There should be one entrance and one exit to keep a proper control on incoming and outgoing users. Doors and windows should be protected by means of wire fabric to avoid any loss of books. The height of the unit book rack should be such that a person of normal height should be able to pick up books from topmost shelf.

(iii) **Future growth** : The library buildings required for the forest office should be planned possibly for 20 to 25 years or even more, keeping in view the rate of stock development, number of readers, future use of microforms etc. The building should be extendable to allow for future growth with minimum of disruption.

(iv) **Flexibility** : In case a change in the library functions takes place, then it should be possible to adjust the layout without carrying out major structural operations. This means interchangeability of all major stock areas, service areas, reading areas and staff areas. There should be no interior load bearing walls but the building should be able to bear stack load anywhere. Uniform standards of lighting, ventilation and flooring are necessary to meet the criteria of interchangeability.

(v) **Area** : There should be enough provision for documents, users, staff (admininstrative and operational), service areas, library tools (such as public catalogue, microfilm reader, Xerox machine, typing etc.)

The library area should have the following provisions :

(1) **Office area** : (a) Librarians Office, (b) Processing section, (c) Periodicals section, (d) Acquisition section.

(2) **Service area** : (a) Reference section, (b) circulation section, (c) Public catalogue/computer Terminal area.

(3) **Stack area** : The entire collection of the library can be organised into the following sub-collections : (a) Reference Collection, (b) General collection, (c) Old periodicals collection, and (d) Current periodicals display area.

(4) **Reading area** : Determining the ratio between the users of the library and the number of seats for them has been a very ticklish task. Of course, the aim of each library is to have as large a number of seats as possible. But a balance has to be struck between the number of users and available space. The norms being followed in various countries and in various libraries vary from 20% to 35%.

Two types of reading areas namely area for **serious study** and area for **general study** should be segregated.

In order to work out the space requirement, the following figures based on ISI standards should be followed :

(i) Documents—150 volumes per square metre

(ii) Library Staff—

(a) Librarian and Deputy Librarian - 30 m^2

(b) Classifier, Cataloguer, accession librarian and maintenance librarian — 9 m^2

(c) Administrative and professional staff not at service points and other than (b) above — 5 m^2.

(iii) Users : Average area per reader in the reading room-2.33 m^2.

(iv) Services : Area required for services to users can be calculated on the basis of local requirements.

(v) Other purposes : Space for other purposes can be called non-assignable space. The space can be calculated for corridors, entrances, lobbies, toilet facilities and transportation etc.

Indian Standard Institution : 1553-1976, has indicated the number of readers, seats and staff which should be provided for different types and sizes of libraries. Therefore it would be possible to make a rough estimate of space requirements. This would help in calculating possible cost of construction.

Equipment and Furniture

The forest library would require the following categories of equipment and furniture :

(I) Movable furniture and equipment

(II) Fixed equipment

(I) Movable Furniture and Equipment

The movable furniture and equipment would consist of the following :

(a) **Items for public areas** : They include tables, chairs, shelving, card catalogues, cabinets, counters and desks, filing cabinets and exhibition cases.

(b) **Items for staff work-rooms** : Office machines (typewriter, stencil duplicator), work-tables, desks, chairs, shelving, charging tray files and book trolleys.

(c) **Equipment for providing specialised services** : They include :

(i) **Electronic typewriter** : It is better than the ordinary typewriter because speed and accuracy is guaranteed. The added advantage is that an electronic typewriter is also bilingual and memory can be retained in casettees.

(ii) **Photocopy machine** : For taking out the copies or extracts from books, periodicals etc. so that new ideas may be circulated and implemented in the field.

(iii) **Computer** : One computer Terminal can be placed near the stack area and another terminal can be placed for the users in the reading area. In future one more computer terminal can be used for issue and return of books.

Computer for on-line catalogue

The on-line revolution is taking place in the field of library management. It is quite significant at the circle and the divisional level. It will lead to qualitative improvement of existing library and information services. It will also become possible to start certain services which are difficult to provide otherwise.

One or more computer terminal can be placed in the library for the users. This will help in (a) cataloguing, (b) retrieval of information, and (c) other services.

On line access to internationally available databases which are not available on CD-ROM can be accessed using Gateway Packet Switching System (GPSS) offered by Videsh Sanchar Nigam Ltd. (VSNL).

The commercial databases, i.e those available on line, or disseminated on CD-ROM or on magnetic tape, have two main advantages. They provide access to a much larger store of information that it would be possible to keep and search efficiently in paper format, and the data can be down loaded on a floppy disckette for further processing of storage. Retrieval of information from CD-ROM is particularly appreciated as search software interfaces are usually very user friendly and users themselves can learn to search for information very quickly. Users often have ideas which they find difficult to express freely in key words, and the ability to browse through information at leisure aids the development of their ideas.

(d) **Additional items :** These would depend upon the requirements of the library.

The purchase of these items will depend upon the adequate finance, shelf capacity, staff etc.

The above lists of items are merely illustrative. In practice, a wide variety of items are available. This can be seen from the items available for storage. Book rack, book display rack, periodicals display rack, periodicals rack, microfilm cabinet, newspaper stand, dictionary stand; filing cabinet for pamphlets, vertical filing cabinet, exhibition cases; and cabinet for maps.

Reading Table : The size of reading room table for a single person should be 900 x 600 mm. The size of reading room table for three readers should be 2400 x 600 mm. The height of table top shall be 750 mm.

Chair : The height of the seat of chair = 430 mm.

effective depth of chair = 450 mm.

Shelving : Metal shelving is preferred because it is generally less costly, more durable and possesses flexibility in adjustment of shelves.

Double faced unit book rack is of size :

height 2175 mm, length 1840 mm ; Depth 460 mm.

Single faced unit book rack has following dimensions :—

height 2175 mm. length 1840 mm. Depth 230 mm .

Card Catalogue Cabinet

Two drawer cabinet made of metal shall have the following dimensions : height 235 mm, width 320 mm, depth 510 mm. Four drawer cabinet of steel shall have the following dimensions : Height 255 mm., Width 320 mm., Depth 510 mm.

Card catalogue cabinets made of wood are preferred over those of steel because metal trays are noisy to handle. The wooden cabinet looks elegant. It is essential that well-seasoned wood alongwith good workmanship should be used :—

The dimensions in mm. are :

No. of trays	Length	Height		Depth
		Stand	Body	
24	1090	840	455	455
20	915	840	455	455
16	710	840	455	455
12	560	710	455	455
9	560	710	455	455

The library furniture should be a aesthetically pleasing with regard to design and finish. For this colors and materials should be coordinated. Such a furniture will make the library an inviting place. The furniture should be economical and easy to maintain. The following references shall be useful :

ISI specification for library furniture and fittings :

Part - I Timber (I. S : 1829 (Part-I) -1978)

ISI Specification for library furniture and fittings :

Part - II Steel (IS : 1829 (Part I) - 1977).

Fixed Equipments

The fixed equipment consists of the following :

(i) **Lighting** : Provision of proper lighting is essential and should be taken into consideration early at the 'building programme' stage. Lighting must be distributed uniformly. It is important to keep in view that stacks must be well lit so as to provide sufficient light for book shelves especially lowest as well as highest ones. Research and Study carrels should have "Some additional functional lighting", arranged besides the general lighting. Required level of illumination should be achieved by combining natural day lighting and the artificial lighting. Use of day lighting will lead to economy.

(ii) **Heating, Cooling & Ventilation** : Proper level of heating, cooling and ventilation can be maintained by airconditioning. Even if it is costly it will invite lot of readers in the library.

(iii) **Noise Prevention** : All types of noises should be avoided and controlled. Noise can be reduced by using insulating materials and devices. Use of proper floor covering can be useful. Equipment or mechanical devices, such as telephones, typewriters, photocopy machine etc. should be kept away from reading areas.

(iv) **Communications** : The devices for communication include booklifts, telephones, fire alarm systems etc.

(v) **Fumigation :** In order to avoid damage to books from insects and fungi, fumigation should be done.

Services Offered by a Library

The following services can be offered by the library.

(1) **Technical Information Dissemination** : A wide range of technical queries received from various parts of the country and abroad can be answered.

(2) **Literature Search Services** : On receiving requests from the scientists a survey of the literature covering a particular subject, and list of the pertinent books, journal articles, reports etc. can be made. Such surveys may either be limited, covering only specified sources or comprehensive, covering all known sources of literature within a specific period, such literature surveys are complied later as bibliographies.

(3) **Resource Sharing Services** : The tremendous growth of the published literature has led to the phenomenon of literature explosion or information explosion. Such a growth has made it very difficult for libraries to maintain comprehensive acquisition of documents as the number of publications to be acquired and also their prices keep on increasing. This has led to the role of Libraries or information centres changing from acquiring comprehensive collections, to providing access to comprehensive collection available in various other libraries or information centres. Thus there can be a reciprocal arrangement for mutual benefit.

(4) **Translation Services** : A substantial portion of forestry literature is published in English which can be translated in Hindi or regional languages. A translation unit can be set up which will also provide interpretation services on request.

(5) **Document Delivery Services** : This will provide reprographic facility capable of supplying excellent reproductions of documents in normal, enlarged or reduced sizes.

The various reprographic services include :—

(a) Supplying photocopies of articles/papers from journals, current as well as back issues available in the library.

(b) Supplying reprints of papers published in Indian and Foreign journals.

(c) Full-size hard copy reproduction of microfiche or microfilms, and

(d) Production of transparencies for overhead projection.

(6) **Micrographic Services** : The use of microfilming equipment can offer the following services :—

(a) Preparation of slides, positive, negative or colour of documents for presentation at symposia/seminars.

(b) Preparation of microfiches of technical reports and proceedings of symposia/seminars etc.

(c) Preparation of microfilms of documents for inter library loan service; and

(d) microfilm readers for reading microfiches, microfilms and microcards.

(7) **Photographic and Video Filming Services** : The services offered include photographic and video filming coverage of important functions, visits of dignitaries, inauguration of symposia/conferences, experimental facilities etc.

(8) **Printing and Binding Services** : This includes following services :

(a) Desk Top Publishing (DTP) for producing camera-ready texts of the publications to be brought out.

(b) Off-set and letter printing.

(c) Paper cutting machines, embossing machine, wire-stitching machine, spiral binding machine and screen printing machine.

(d) Printing of invitations cards for inaugural functions of a symposia / seminars, visiting cards etc. can also be done on platen letterpress printing machine.

23

Constraints and Remedies for Proper Functioning of Forest Libraries

The feasibility of eastablishing and renovating reference libraries at the forest offices would facilitate the development of forestry education. At the same time it would ensure that subordinate staffs are technically competent to do their field jobs with a clear understanding of what is expected of them in the changing scenario of present day multi-faceted environmental problems.

It is a matter of natural consequence that libraries will and must be located at the headquarters of senior level forest officers who are expected to make maximum use of analytical characters and interpretations. Presently the existing libraries are in the miniature state.

The libraries should be well equipped and managed in such a way that all the five laws of library science are satisfied :

1. Books are for use,
2. Every reader his book,
3. Every book its reader,
4. Save the time of the reader,
5. A library is a growing organisation.

Accordingly the work flow chart in a library is expressed as :

Withdrawal — Documentation — Maintenance — Reference

service — Circulation — Classification & Cataloguing — Accessioning — Periodicals – Ordering — Book selection.

The following are the constraints and their remedies suggested for the proper functioning of the forest libraries :

(1) **Lack of Space** : The present space available to the libraries in the Forest Department are generally insufficient. Therefore bigger halls should be provided or newly constructed to accommodate the requisite number of books, periodicals, display rack, issue counter and reading place of room to the users.

(2) **Lack of Staff** : There is lack of staff in the library. As proposed the staff should be diverted to the libraries to provide various services in the library. The staff should be trained in library science.

(3) **Lack of Books or Stock** : There is lack of desired and latest books. Books should be made available in local languages also. There should be sufficient number of volumes of text books, reference books, new books, and popular publications.

(4) **Lack of proper cataloguing** : The cataloguing should be done as per "Oxford System of Decimal Classification for Forestry" Presently the classification is incomplete and is being done as Accession numberwise. There is dearth of good catalogue and catalogue cards. The cataloguing should be done on three lines according to , (a) Class No. (b) Title and (c) Author, so that retrieval is quick and effective.

(5) **Lack of good service** : The Posting of sufficient staff will ensure all the services in a better way.

(6) **Acquisition Policy** : There should be a 'book selection committee' for book acquisitioning. All the publishers catalogue should be obtained and checked. The book-selection should be unbiased and errors in book selection should be avoided.

(7) **Withdrawal and shelf capacity** : The books that are of no use and are unnecessarily occupying the library shelves should be removed, to avoid problem of shelf capacity.

(8) **Lack of Furniture and Equipment** : There is utter lack of display racks, book shelves, tables, chairs and other furnitures and equipments. The library should be airconditioned. Similarly a photocopy machine should be provided for xeroxing important pages and circulating it to the staff.

(9) **Lack of Publicity** : The important books, periodicals etc. should be exhibited and displayed in an effective manner. The list of new and important books should be circulated regularly to the staff because those who are outstationed in Ranges, Rounds and Beats can not come frequently to consult the library.

(10) **Suggestion Book** : A suggestion book should be kept in each library.

(11) **Lack of Funds** : There is lack of funds. Better funds will improve the library drastically. The library building should be made fully equipped. Similarly funds should be provided for selection, acquisition, accessioning, classifying, and cataloguing.

(12) **Lack of interest in reading** : The users or staff are yet to develop interest in forestry literature. In absence of reading habit the work performance is mainly guided by age old practices rather than by latest scientific knowledge.

ANNEXURE — I

Some of the Good Libraries in India

(1) Bhabha Atomic Research Centre, Library and Information Services (Anushakti Nagar), Mumbai.

(2) Bharat Heavy Electricals Limited, Hyderabad, A.P.

(3) Central Building Research Institute Library (Roorkee) U.P.

(4) Central Leather Research Institute Library (Chennai).

(5) Central Food Technological Research Institute Library, (Mysore).

(6) Central Machine Tools Institute, National Information Centre for Machine Tools and Production Engineering (Bangalore).

(7) Central Road Research Institute Library (New Delhi).

(8) Indian Institute of Public Administration Library, (New Delhi.

(9) Indian Institute of Science Library, Bangalore.

(10) Indian Standards Institution Technical Library (New Delhi).

(11) Indian Institute of Technology (at Kanpur, Chennai, Mumbai).

(12) Indian Statistical Institute Library. (Calcutta).

(13) National Library, Calcutta.

(14) National Aeronautical Laboratory Information Centre for Aeronautics (Bangalore).

(15) National Chemical Laboratory, Library and Documentation Services (Pune).

(16) National Medical Library (New Delhi).

(17) National Science Library (New Delhi).

(18) Nehru Memorial Museum and Library (New Delhi).

(19) Physical Research Laboratory Library, Ahmedabad.

(20) Regional Research Centre Library, Kalpakkam.

(21) Tata Institute of Fundamental Research (Mumbai).

Many of these libraries have computer facilities. Some of the libraries have access to international data bases abroad. For example, BHEL (Hyderabad) has online access to DIALOG system. National Aeronautical Laboratory has access to European Space Agency Computer at Frascati (Rome).

ANNEXURE — II

Some useful abbreviations for Library

A–1900;		A50—1950
A & I	—	Abstracting and Indexing.
AACR 2	—	Anglo American Cataloguing Rules (2nd)
AC	—	Author Catalogue; AR—Annual Report.
CAS	—	Current Awareness Service.
CC	—	Card Catalogue.
CCC	—	Classified Catalogue Code.
CP	—	Conference Proceedings.
CCS	—	Circulation Control System.
CL	—	Control Library.
DL	—	Depository Library.
DTP	—	Desk Top Publishing.
FA	—	Forestry Abstracts.
GPSS	—	Gateway Packet Switching System.
ICDD	—	International Centre for Diffraction Data.
LISD	—	Library & Information Services Division.
PC-PDF	—	Power Diffraction File Card Retrieval/Display System.
RADU	—	Recent Annual Display Unit.
ROM	—	Read only Memory.
SDI	—	Selective Dissemination of Information.
TR	—	Technical Reports.
UDC	—	Universal Decimal Classification.
VSNL	—	Videsh Sanchar Nigam Ltd.
WTI	—	World Translation Index (The Netherlands)

Bibliography

Anduron, A.J. ed., Problems in Library Management-Littleton, Co. Libraries Unlimited, 1981, pp. 282.

Advances in Librarianship, Vol 7, Ed by Melvin 3, Voigt and Michael H. Harris, London Academic Press, 1977.

Boaz, Martha. ed., Towards the improvement of Library education, Colorado, Libraries Unlimited, 1973, pp. 168.

Bose, H., Universal Decimal Classification. Theory and practice, Sterling Publications Pvt. Ltd. New Delhi, 1990, pp. 190.

Borko, H., Towards a theory of indexing. Inf. Process management 13 (1977).

Carnovsky, Leon ed., The medium size public library, its status and future ed. by Leon Carnovsky and Howard W. Winger, Illinois, University of Chicago Press, 1963, pp. 142.

Collison RL Ed., Progress in Library Science, London Butterworths 1967, pp. 222.

Corbett, Edmund V., An introduction to Librarianship, 2nd ed. revised and enlarged – London, Clarke, and Co. 1969, pp. 442.

Colin Harrison and Rosemary Beenham, Basics of Librarianship, 2nd ed. London, Clive Bingley, 1985.

Dehlberg, I, Major Development in Classification — Advances in Librarianship V-7 (1977), 12-92.

Dougherty, Richard H., Scientific management of library operations by Richard M. Dougherty and Fred. J. Heinrnity, New York, The Scarecrow Press, 1966, pp. 258.

Enright B.J., New media and the library in education, London Clive Bingley 1972; 162 pp.

Foskett, A.C., Universal Decimal Classification, London. Clive Bingley, 1973, pp. 172.

Ford, Stephen, The Acquisition of library materials, Chicago A.L.A. 1974; pp. 237.

Gelfand, M.A., Universities libraries for developing countries — Paris, UNESCO, 1971, pp. 158.

Guide to Universal Decimal Classification - BS 1000 C.— 1963 (FID 345), London, BSI, 1963, pp. 128.

Guy R. Lyle, Administration of the College Library 4th ed. New York, H.W. Wilson, 1974.

Hickey, Doral Yn J., Problems in organising library collections, New York, R.R. Bowker, 1972, pp. 206.

Hidson, Richard, Reflection on the utilization of the Universal Decimal Classification - Aslib proc. 31 (6) June, 1979, 305-311.

Holroyd, Gileon ed., Studies in Library Management - London, Clive Bingley, 1974. pp. 167.

Indian Library Association, Libraries and the Book Trade ; Seminar papers presented at the All India Seminar held in Feb., 1982, New Delhi, pp. 111.

Jones, K.P., Towards a theory of indexing, J. Dnc 32 (1978). pp. 122.

Krishan Kumar, Library Administration and Management 1993, Vikas Publishing House Pvt. Ltd. Jangpura, New Delhi pp. 200

Krishan Kumar, Library Organisation-1993, Vikas Publishing House Pvt. Ltd. Jangpura-New Delhi. pp. 278.

Lucille . Strauss et al., Scientific and Technical libraries 2nd ed. New York, Beeker and Hayes, 1972.

Mill J., Modern Outline of Library Classification, Bombay, Asia, 1962, pp. 143.

Molgard, Hansen, R. and Rigby, Med. Seminar on UDC in mechanised information retrieval system, Copenhagen, 2-6, September (1968) Proceedings. (FID / CR Report No. 9).

Mukherjee, A.K., Librarianship ; its Philosophy and history, Bombay, Asia, 1966. pp. 220.

Oxford system of Decimal Classification in Forestry, Authorised English version March – 1954; CAB International Commonwealth Agricultural Bureaux, Farnham Royal England - U.K. pp. 115.

Palmer, Richard Phillips — Case Studies in library Computer systems, New York, R.R. Bonoker, 1973, p. 214.

Ranganathan, S.R., Five laws of Library Science, Madras, Library Association, 1957.

Ranganathan, S.R., Prolegomeha to library classification Ed. 3 Asia Publishing, 1967 (Ranganathan series in Library Science, 20).

Ranganathan, S.R., Library Book Selection - Sarada Ranganathan Endowment for Library Science, Bangalore, UBS Publishers' Distributors Ltd. Ansari Road, New Delhi. 1992, p. 436.

Sahai, Shrinath, Library and Community - New Delhi. Today and Tomorrows Book Agency. Some Problems of General Classification Schemes - Report of a conference held in London, June, 1963, London, Library Association, 1964.

Setty K. Umapathy, Problems in library management, New Delhi, Vikas, 1976, p. 111.

Sharma, Chandra Kanta, University Library, its management and organisation, New Delhi, Metropolitan Book Co., 1977, p. 172.

Universal Decimal Classification, Abridged English Edition Ed. 3, BS, 1000 A ; 1961.

Wilson L.R. and Tauber M.F., University library, 2nd ed. New York, Columbia University Press, 1964.

Zachert, Martha Jane K, Simulation teaching of Library administration, New York, R.R. Bowker, 1975, p. 297.

Index

2

Introduction to Classification

Classification Systems

The several classification systems that exist can be enumerated as under :

(1) *Special* : Used for covering a particular subject or laying emphasis on it.

(2) *Scientific* : Used for systematic study of the phenomena of the natural world.

(3) *General* : This system is used for displaying all recorded knowledge or the universe of information.

This is further sub-divided as below :—

(a) *Enumerative Classification* : Comprises categories in which the universe of knowledge is divided and exhaustively listed.

(b) *Faceted or analytical-Synthetic Classification* : Characteristics common to many categories are identified. These are then arranged into lists (or tables) each of which represents a facet. Subjects are thus analysed into their elements, which can later be recombined or synthesised by the user.

(c) *Aspect Classification* : Phenomena of the natural world are classified against the perspective of discipline or context in which they appear.

(4) Documentary : Used for the management of documents for

[illegible]

lished in twenty-three languages of the world.

The Classification Research Group (CRG) of U.K. formed in 1952 is responsible for the faceted scheme which is supposed to break a new ground. This scheme is based on the facet analysis of Ranganathan. The Universal Decimal Classification Scheme is in fact, the first analytic - synthetic scheme which displays faceted structure. The Colon Classification (1963) in which analysis has found practical application in minute detail, is said to have, in turn, drawn its inspiration from U.D.C. Scheme.